putting up
more

putting up
more

A Guide to Canning Jams, Relishes, Chutneys, Pickles, Sauces, and Salsas

Stephen Palmer Dowdney

Photographs by Rick McKee

GIBBS SMITH
TO ENRICH AND INSPIRE HUMANKIND

First Edition
15 14 13 12 11   5 4 3 2 1

Published by
Gibbs Smith, Publisher
P.O. Box 667
Layton, Utah 84041

1.800.748.5439 orders
www.gibbs-smith.com

Cover design by Renee Bond
Interior design by Debra McQuiston
Printed and bound in Hong Kong
Gibbs Smith books are printed on paper produced from sustainable PEFC-certified forest/controlled wood source. Learn more at www.pefc.org.

Library of Congress Cataloging-in-Publication Data

Dowdney, Stephen Palmer.
 Putting up more : a guide to canning jams, relishes, chutneys, pickles, sauces, and salsas / Stephen Dowdney ; photographs by Rick McKee.
— 1st ed.
    p. cm.
 Includes index.
 ISBN 978-1-4236-0739-7
 1. Canning and preserving. I. Title.
 TX603.D694 2011
 641.4—dc22
                        2010034120

To Thomas Heyward Dowdney, best friend and confidant, business partner and son, who worked side by side with me for so many years as we struggled to give to our community the best put-up products anywhere in America, I dedicate this book.

contents

acknowledgments

WRITING A BOOK is much like sketching the lines for a new automobile. From a sleek drawing to putting in the key, turning on the ignition, and driving off in a car that will hopefully be a marketing success by meeting so many of a population's wants, dreams, and demands, is a monumental undertaking—with the drawing being just one action.

For me, that action would never have been if it were not for Christopher Robbins, CEO of Gibbs Smith, and his belief in me that I could do it one more time. Thank you, Christopher! And then there is my editor, Linda Nimori. I appreciate more than words can describe her steadfast attitude not to silence even my tiniest peep but rather to force me to say what I wanted within her space confines. Thank you, Linda, thank you! There are fifty-one professionals at "The Barn," as Gibbs Smith calls his headquarters, and the Distribution Center. Every person has and plays a part and, although I might not know their names, I know of their work. Theirs is of the highest caliber I have ever witnessed in any industry. I am grateful to be included as part of such a team.

Layout can often determine the success of a project such as this. I attribute much of the success of my first book to the way that Debra McQuiston designed it. I have the utmost faith that this book will be equally judged as perfectionism to the "nth" degree.

There is no better test of a recipe than to sample and attempt to sell it. My business partner at the local farmers markets does this for me. Without Lee Lambert, I would find myself operating in a vacuum much of the time. He tastes and gives his opinion, plus I know what he REALLY thinks when he talks up a new product. Further, it is not so easy for an artist (of sorts) to promote his own work. I find it, well, embarrassing. Lee is like my gallery manager. I could not ask for a finer marketer.

And then there is the "crew," that group of friends who is willing to offer more than a "don't quit your day job" as criticism, like the friend who suggests the addition of this and the removal of that, it's too sweet or not sweet enough, use balsamic not cider, and so forth. Every recipe needs tweaking, and Pamela was definitely the tweaker. Always after the initial recipe is set, my first guinea pig is my mother. Sometimes it's difficult to get her to criticize my work, but she does have her subtle Southern ways, like the time she said, "Well, Steve, it sure looks beautiful in the jar!" To all these professionals and friends, I give a very big thank you, for without each and every one of you, this book would not be. Thanks again!

— introduction —

CANNING IS A SCIENCE; canning is an art. Canning requires a bit of common sense, the ability to read, and the willingness to follow instructions; to know and understand the very basics of culinary discipline—like how to peel a carrot or chop an onion without peeling or chopping a finger. The really good news is that the art of canning requires a minimum amount of study, the understanding of only a few very basic concepts, and a willingness to spend the time necessary to create products that will have and hold a fresh flavor unlike anything that can be purchased anywhere, regardless of price. If this might be you and your desire, then become a student—and welcome to a new world. After a few pages and your first foray into the world of "putting things up," you and your family's dining life will change forever and for the better.

There are two distinctly different canning modalities: low acid and acid/acidified. Low acid involves a procedure where higher than boiling temperatures, produced by steam under pressure, heat a product for a specified time and temperature to produce a safe and sterile product. The process involves pressure vessels, extreme heat, and critical timing. The home preserver using this method is often putting away raw produce for use later in the year. This might work for a handful of garden varieties, but the majority of basic put-up produce requires such high heat applications that even out-of-season, fresh, store-bought imports are a better, more nutritious, and often the less expensive course. Consequently, I do not recommend this method for standard canning practices.

The second is acid and/or acidified mixtures, a method where jarred recipes are sterilized and rendered safe by a combination of an acid level, a temperature that is lower than boiling water, and a vacuum. This method of canning involves a process where the home preserver prepares for storage-completed recipes using fresh, ripe-harvested, often local, produce. There is no equal to such preserved jars, and this becomes the focus of *Putting Up More*.

Nearly half the meals eaten in the United States are consumed away from home or are made with foods commercially prepared. Fast food is unhealthy, restaurant food is expensive, and prepared foods for home consumption are most often produced with the lowest-bid commodities or, put bluntly, the cheapest stuff available. The problem compounds further because gourmet home cooking takes skill, talent, and often lots of training. And preparation takes time, often more time than is available; plus, fancy meals are expensive to prepare, very expensive. Home canning ushers in a successful alternative. Home "put up" recipes like many in this book and in the previous volume, *Putting Up,* can turn the simplest of fares into exciting "restaurant-grade" presentations while affording superior dining experiences. Along with the recipes in this book are many personal successes and best uses for each along with a step-by-step narrative.

But the advantage of home preserving isn't just for dining. When family members get involved in the canning process, not only do they build a ready-made pantry of relishes, pickles, preserves, sauces, and soups to enhance what otherwise might be just another lackluster meal, they create an activity spanning from the harvest or purchase of produce, to preparing and readying the recipe, to finally going through the canning process. There are tasks aplenty for almost all ages and activities that build unity, strengthening the family bond. I cannot tell you the numbers of people from all over the country who come to our local farmers market booths to sample, only to begin reflecting (sometimes with a tear) upon the days of their youth with a parent or grandparent. They speak as if those were the best times of their childhood, and they might well have been. The simple art of canning can do that for a family, for it binds them close from field to table!

There was a time not so long ago when families dined and entertained at home. Weekend dinner parties were common occurrences. Friends got together and enjoyed each other's company, conversation, and food. During the workweek, breakfasts and suppers were important family times. These mealtimes provided a special closeness and a very personal education unique to each family unit. For the children, it was an extra and beneficial training exercise, for as they listened to parents discuss the day, they learned how to conduct their lives. And for those young minds, sharing their day and their trials while getting advice and counsel firmly integrated them as family participants and built their integrity.

We have traveled far from those easier times and fine family standards. If we take a moment to look back at the 1950s, '60s, '70s, and even the early '80s, this was the way. Life was simple and filled with purpose. Somewhere along the journey, maybe wanting more time and money caused us to forsake the simple rules of living. But natural forces have their way. Today, when single dollars are again meaningful, are fewer, and have farther to go, the process begins to reverse. Where once we all dined out too often or ate separately, eating at home together is "lookin'" good!

Putting Up More is intended to provide exceptional recipes for home canning, and it contains many breakfast, lunch, dinner, and snack suggestions utilizing the recipes you have preserved and stored in the pantry. Each time you open a jar, you might be lending dignity

to what otherwise could have been a common nibble. Even quick, inexpensive, and simple home cooking will become the adventure that dining out used to be, and restaurants once again will become reserved for that very special occasion.

Background

I was first exposed to the art of canning by observing my grandmother. She not only put up recipes for the family but also had a successful commercial cannery business. After attempting just about everything one might do in a lifetime, I returned to my roots with my son, and we began working together side by side. For twelve years we owned and operated the premier South Carolina "small batch" cannery. When it comes to canning, we know our stuff. We specialized in original old time Southern recipes, the put-up jars that once graced farmers' breakfast tables, Southern sideboards, and dinner tables. Our company and its products have been featured on numerous radio and television shows; in local, regional, and national newspapers; in magazines and books. We were never able to meet all the demands for our products simply because we refused go the way of commercialism. Using only the freshest vine-ripened produce, the best fresh herbs, and the finest and often the most expensive ingredients, we wanted our products to taste just like a grandmother's efforts, and they did. My first volume, *Putting Up*, featured all those wonderful Southern recipes. In the same tradition, this volume offers a host of new recipes created with produce available to all from around our nation and beyond.

Help as Needed

Anyone can preserve fine recipes. It just takes a little reading, studying, some understanding, a small standard stocked kitchen, and a few specific canning items—thankfully, all inexpensive. If you cannot find locally what you search, in the back of this volume is a resource section. It is designed to help with your needs and wants as they pertain to canning. From dried herbs and spices to equipment and canning glass, it is all there.

Sometimes folks new to the canning process become overwhelmed. Like taking any first step, it can be scary. But, just to be sure, a friend with know-how is probably nearer than you might think. And if not, don't fret; help is just a website away. Feel free to ask me. I have an active website containing a specific section devoted just to canning and the two books I have written. I always attempt to respond promptly.

Canning Science

This volume is intended to be a companion to my first book, *Putting Up*. In that book, I wrote about canning safety measures in intricate detail along with the whys of each. This not only provided a bastion of safe canning practices but also imparted the knowledge to allow a home canner to safely create or prepare and preserve recipes beyond what are found in books or the already tried. In this book, I have omitted many of those details so as not to be redundant; however, I still have provided all the essentials for safe, controlled, precision canning. These are the same safety measures the Food and Drug Administration requires of all commercial canneries. For the home canner, these simple measures and tests will ensure a safe and worry-free canning experience. They are for your safety; it is imperative that you use them!

Preserving Methods

There are many ways of preserving fruits and vegetables: drying, freezing, and canning. When one combines multiple ingredients to create an acid or acidified recipe to be preserved by canning, one of two systems is used.

HOT PACKING is by far the easiest canning system and is the one most often used. After the ingredients are prepared, placed in a pot, cooked to the proper consistency, and brought to the correct temperature as described in a recipe, the product is scooped from the pot, poured into sterile jars, and filled to the fill ring or canning line (a molded circular ring just below the lid threads). Last, a sterile lid is applied, tightened, and the jar inverted for a minimum of 2 minutes.

WATER BATHING is used when hot packing will not work. When a recipe calls for large chunks of produce, like dill pickles for example, it becomes unfeasible to pour the hot ingredients into jars. Therefore, the jars are packed with the solids of the recipe by hand and are then placed in a jar holding rack that is part of a water bath system. The liquid pickling solution is heated to boiling and then poured into each jar just to the canning line, no further. This is most important because liquids will expand as they heat. If the liquids flow over the top, the ability to seal will be impaired.

The center jar, known as the cold jar because it is always filled first, will hold a thermometer inserted thru a temporary makeshift lid with a small hole in the center (a 1-minute homemade project). The remaining jars, usually six, are loosely capped with sterile lids so air can flow out; once tightened, an excellent vacuum can be created as the jars cool. The rack is lowered slowly and carefully into the boiling water bath. The water level in the bath cannot go beyond the fill rings, or canning lines. Again, this is critical when water bathing because one cannot allow water to enter the loosely sealed jars. The water in the bath will stop boiling as the jars are lowered in. At the first signs of boiling, lower the heat slightly to prevent bubbling water from entering the loosely capped jars. When the prescribed temperature for the recipe is reached, wait 2 additional minutes before removing the rack. Once out of the bath, tighten each jar's lid, replace the lid on the center jar, and finally invert all jars for a minimum of 2 minutes.

Safe Canning Practices

With both hot packing and water bathing, there are four requirements that must be met to always ensure a finished product is free of bacteria, will remain free of bacteria, and will be safe to ingest: sterilization, vacuum, acidity, and temperature.

STERILIZATION: Bacteria-free workspaces, utensils, and equipment, as well as canning jars and lids are essential. This is accomplished by sterilization. In days past, boiling water was used to complete some parts of this feat, and it was time-consuming. The way the FDA requires a commercial canner to sterilize is through the use of sodium hypochlorite mixed with water, a solution of 200 parts per million. The home canner can accomplish this by mixing one-quarter cup of bleach containing 6-percent sodium hypochlorite for each 2 gallons of water in a sink. At the time of this writing, a quarter cup of Clorox meets this requirement. Always make a deep enough solution to cover upright standing jars. Using a clean dishcloth wetted in the solution, wipe all working surfaces.

Jars and canning lids must be clean and free of bacteria before canning. The best way to accomplish this is to wash both and rinse them well before soaking the jars upright in

the sterilizing solution for 2 minutes. Afterwards, the jars should drain upside down on the sterile countertop until ready for filling.

As for the lids, the center section of a two-piece canning lid must be new, never used before, and the only part that must be sterile; the easiest way is to put the lids with their associated rings in a colander, submerge for 2 minutes, and put aside to drain. Once the process is complete, put the canning tools in the bleach water for 2 minutes. Last, rinse and wring the cloth for a second time in the sterile solution because it will be used again later to clean jar rims that get fouled during the canning process (more on this later).

VACUUM: A vacuum is created when the hot matter in the jar shrinks as it cools. The vacuum is maintained because new canning lids (again, never reuse lids) have a rubberized seal that marries airtight to the jar lids. When inverted for 2 or more minutes, the jars will be sealed. The hot product softens the rubber, which assists in molding the seal to the jar. If the rim of a canning jar is not chipped or otherwise damaged and is not contaminated with bits of recipe matter left by the funnel or by a drip (this is the function of the bleach cloth), and if the lid is new and the jar is filled to the canning line, then an excellent and proper vacuum will form as the product cools, keeping the preserved product safe, without mold, and fresh-tasting for several years. To see if a good seal has been created, tap the top center of each jar with the back of a teaspoon after the jars have cooled completely. A jar that has not sealed will have a completely different sound than a sealed jar. If a jar has failed to seal and if it is 24 hours or less since canning, the errant jar can be refrigerated and it will be fine. I always perform this vacuum test before I open a jar for the final pH test, if one is required by the recipe (more on this coming up).

ACIDITY (pH): pH stands for "potential of hydrogen." It is a measure of acidity. A pH of 7 is considered neutral. Below 7 is acidic and above is basic, or alkaline. pH is by far the most critical factor when canning. Regardless of what is being preserved by water bath or by hot pack, the combined pH can NEVER exceed 4.6. There are NO exceptions. If it does, a deadly toxin can form. Botulinum is one of the world's most lethal poisons, and there is no way to detect its presence.

When canning jars have cooled, the vacuum that forms creates a "no oxygen" environment (or, technically said, an anaerobic environment), the ground necessary for the toxin's generation. Botulinum is odorless and tasteless, and it does not cause lids to bulge like some people believe. Bulging lids are caused from other bacteria because of improper canning practices, like improperly sealed lids, improper canning temperatures (too low), or non-sterile jars or lids.

Further compounding the challenge, produce once safe to put up may no longer be presumed safe. Advancements created by genetic engineering have altered the pH levels of some fruits and vegetables. Since the first cans of tomatoes were sealed, tomatoes fell into a pH range of approximately 3.8 to 4.5; today, one can purchase a near pH 7 (low acid) tomato. Therefore, it becomes more than just prudent to test every finished product that is specified as acidified in the recipe notes with the exception of acidified, sugar saturated, a group where large amounts of sugar reduce the internal water content of vegetables, thus ensuring safety against botulinum. This is a special category reserved for pepper jellies and certain jams. All others get tested, no exceptions!

The recipes in this book are safe. They all fall well below the 4.6 level, allowing for significant margins of error. Still, an ingredient can get forgotten when a phone is answered, vinegar with a less than the standard 5 percent acidity gets inadvertently used, a tomato that has a pH below 4.6 gets replaced with a genetically engineered low-acid tomato. Things happen. Testing prevents mishap. Just before a recipe is canned is the time to make the first pH test. This is called the preliminary pH test.

• **Hot-pack method: just before canning, take a small tear of a test paper and read the pH by comparing the color to the chart. If it is too high, follow the instructions in the recipe canning notes to rectify.**

• **Water-bath method: test the pH of the liquid in the center (cold) jar. If it is too high, something is missing in the recipe, or low-acid or diluted vinegar was used. See the recipe's canning notes for guidance.**

In both water bath and hot pack methods, a final pH test needs to be performed after twenty-four hours when the product has cooled and the acids and bases have all combined. For hot pack items, this is easy. Open a jar, dip in the paper, and test. For water bath products, the solids need to be rinsed with distilled water, crushed in a solution of distilled water, and the results of the water read. In the back of this book, you will find a source for purchasing pH paper and pH meters. Do not attempt to put up acidified foods without testing.

TEMPERATURE: The higher the temperature, the more bacteria gets killed, at least to a point. The canning temperature of a recipe is ultimately determined by the pH of the whole, or the combined acidity created by all ingredients in the recipe. The table below shows the minimum safe canning temperature based upon acidity. I always add 3 degrees when hot-packing to account for the cooling caused by the hot product flowing into a cool jar.

MAXIMUM PH	MINIMUM DEGREES F
3.9 and lower	182 degrees F
4.1	185 degrees F
4.2	190 degrees F
4.3	195 degrees F
4.4	205 degrees F
4.5	210 degrees F

NOTE: I use pH paper as well as sophisticated testing equipment; yet, I never, Never, NEVER can anything above pH 4.2. Instead, I bring the pH down to my personal, comfortable safe level.

Canning Basics

1. Don't rush. If one does not have time to finish a project at leisure, it is best not to begin. Haste can lead to real problems when canning.

2. Use only jars specifically designed for canning. Preserving jars are tough. They can take the rapid change from cold to hot. The sealing surface is machined to ensure a perfect seal. Although they are initially expensive, they can be used over and over. They are worth the extra money.

3. Canning lids (the center section if using two-piece lids) may be used only once. Packs of twelve replacement lids are available at almost all stores selling canning jars. At discount stores, they sell for about a dollar. The outer ring of the two-piece lid is more expensive than the flat center disc but can be used many times, so be sure to save them. Furthermore, they can be removed after twenty-four hours, minimum.

4. Pick or buy locally when able and only use the freshest, ripest produce available. This is the single greatest key to making products that are superior to other products.

5. Get organized before the process begins. Create the sterile workplace and sterilize all jars and lids. Prepare the produce; have other ingredients out, measured, and ready to use. Count the number of ingredients in the recipe and the number on the counter as a cross check. As each ingredient is used, clear away any remainder or containers like measuring cups. When the counter is again empty, the recipe should be complete.

6. Calibrate the canning thermometer once a month to ensure you are measuring at the correct temperature. (See section below on Specialized Equipment, page 23.)

7. Have pH paper ready for performing the initial pH test as the product comes to temperature. When visible, it means the test will not be forgotten.

8. Consider the canning process as separate from recipe preparation:

   a. Turn the jars right side up.

   b. Get the lids organized (in the rings) and ready.

   c. Have the canning funnel nearby at ready.

   d. Hot packs:

- Perform the initial pH test.
- Fill jars, seal, and invert.

   e. Water baths:

- Place loaded jars in water bath rack.
- Fill center jar or assigned cold jar with the solution first, then fill the others.
- Check pH of center jar liquid by removing a teaspoonful and testing.
- Place special homemade lid on cold jar and insert thermometer.
- Loosely fit the lids to the remaining jars and lower them into the bath with water not exceeding the canning or fill line.
- When temperature is reached, wait 2 minutes, carefully remove jars from water bath, replace thermometer lid, tighten all lids, and invert jars for 2 minutes.

Specialized Equipment

There are a few items that are unique to canning. I'll address only those items not found in a commonly stocked home kitchen. The good news is, when combined, these unique canning items are not expensive, and most should be locally available.

POTS: Generally, a recipe is designed around six to eight jars of finished product, and often one is able to double the recipe; therefore, a large pot is desirable. Not any metal pot will do. The pot used for mixing and heating a recipe must be nonreactive or, more simply put, stainless, enameled iron, or copper with the interior clad of tin or stainless steel. Aluminum and raw cast iron are excellent heat conductors but are taboo for canning because acid reacts with either metal. A stainless pot with a thick conductive metal bottom sandwiched in works great and, if affordable, thick-sandwiched sides will distribute heat even better. I use two pots, a 12-quart and a 22-quart stainless steel, each with a thick-sandwiched bottom only. I found these most reasonability priced at Walmart. They work just fine.

WATER BATH SYSTEM: This "system" is comprised of a flimsy enameled pot and a galva-nized rack. Kits come in several sizes, each made specifically for quarts, pints, or half pints. Be sure to purchase the correct size. The kits are available most anywhere can-ning supplies are sold. I hate to keep pushing a store that has destroyed so many "ma and pa" industries, but I got mine at Walmart. Online, there are stores that sell just the racks. There are also some upscale units on the market. One does not have to purchase a system. Often I use a pot that has a deep-set steamer insert because it holds more jars. The important thing to remember about any water bath process is that the jars cannot touch the bottom of the pot. The one advantage of a rack is the ease of handling. It does make a difference.

THERMOMETER: A chef's pocket meat thermometer is perfect, but it must be the kind that is adjustable. Don't bother with digital; they are not adjustable. Get one with a dial that has a hex nut on the back for adjusting. Submerge the meter's probe at least halfway into distilled boiling water, wait a few seconds until the needle has stabilized, and read. Adjust to 212 degrees if you live at sea level. If you don't, adjust according to the chart below.

ALTITUDE & TEMPERATURE AT WHICH WATER BOILS

Sea level	212 degrees F
1,000 feet	210 degrees F
2,000 feet	208 degrees F
3,000 feet	206 degrees F
4,000 feet	205 degrees F
5,000 feet	203 degrees F
6,000 feet	201 degrees F

Pure water (distilled) boils at the levels above when at altitude; however, if one needs a higher temperature than can be achieved naturally when water bathing, add some salt to the water to increase the boiling point. Just for the record, seawater boils at 218 degrees. The extra 6 degrees will give all the heat needed up to 6,000 feet, not that you'll find a bunch of seawater at 6,000 feet, but one can replicate seawater by adding 6½ tablespoons of salt per gallon of water. Another way is to reduce the water bath temperature necessary by increasing the acidity of the recipe slightly. Most of this is a moot point because, for safety's sake, nobody should be canning at pH 4.4 or above anyway. Again I reiterate, my maximum safe, self-imposed limit for home canning is 4.2. I stick to this like religion.

SPATULA: I consider this specialized because it might be different from what many kitchens have. I use a metal, perfectly flat-tipped, rounded-edge spatula like commercial grills have for flipping burgers. Used to stir the pot, the flat tip ensures all matter on the bottom is shifted so there will be no burning. The curved edges pick up the stuff along the curved edges of the pot. I have perfected a motion that sweeps around the bottom and sides, especially careful to catch the edges, then zigzags across the bottom, leaving no area to burn. Burnt taste gets canned right along with all the good flavors. Stirring correctly is a most important part of canning.

pH PAPER: This might sound like canning is getting complex, but it is not. I buy rolls of short-range 3.4 to 4.8 pH paper. Test strips are more expensive and the range is not as tight. I purchase mine directly from the manufacturer (see resource section on page 170). Tear off a small section about 2 inches in length and dip the strip in the product to test the pH before canning. Compare the color on the tear against the color chart provided with the paper.

After 24 hours do a more comprehensive test. When hot packing, I put up a very small jar (4 ounces) right along with my regular canning just for this purpose. For water bath products, test the liquid before canning. If okay, continue. You'll need to open a jar for the 24-hour test. Place a tiny amount of the canned product rinsed with distilled water in a small bowl, mash completely, add distilled water, mix well, and test. As long as the indication falls below pH 4.3, it is safe and has a significant margin of error; it will be within the pH guidelines of the recipe, and the product will have the correct acidity flavor.

pH METER: Not a requirement, but for those of us who want extreme accuracy and further peace of mind, meters are available and are reasonably priced. The Food and Drug Administration requires commercial canners to use pH meters instead of paper when canning over pH 4.0. This is a bit extreme, but like someone once commented, it's not their money!

CANNING JARS AND LIDS: Not any jar will do. A canning jar is constructed using tempered glass that can quickly expand and contract without breaking. The neck of the jar is separately constructed and fused to the body. It provides a very smooth machined surface to make contact with the rubbery lid material, thus providing a good seal and, consequently, a good vacuum. There is a molded ring around the base of the throat of the jar called the canning line, or fill line. This is unique to canning jars; located just below the threading, it is there to remind the canner of minimum level for a good vacuum and maximum level for water bath products, and represents the exact liquid quantity the jar is deemed to hold.

CANNING FUNNEL: Generally made from plastic, although I have owned a few fancy stainless ones, these funnels have a large throat that snuggly fits into a canning jar. They provide three services: they keep the product going into the jar instead of onto the canning table; they keep the edge of the jar from getting contaminated with product that may later prevent a good seal; and, lastly, when the jar is filled to a point inside the throat of the funnel, the contents of the jar have reached the correct fill level.

WEIGHING SCALE: Food scales are expensive, but a scale is necessary occasionally. Using a less expensive postal scale will work perfectly. A good one for kitchen use weighs from 0 to 4 pounds. It is accurate and will serve the purpose.

Specialized Ingredients

VINEGARS: Not all vinegars are alike. The two most common varieties you'll see are white (also called distilled) and cider. Both MUST be 5 percent acidity to perform correctly when used for canning. Below 5 percent and the final pH might be too high, maybe even lethal. Cider vinegar not only must be 5 percent, it must be made from real apples. Watch for the word "flavored" as a dead giveaway that the stuff is a fake. Fake cider vinegar defeats the purpose of home canning. When we can junk, we get junk! One might as well buy commercial. Some of the recipes in this book use balsamic vinegar. This is a very special, very flavorful vinegar. It is expensive but delicious. Usually the acid percentage is higher, often 6 percent or greater. The recipes in this book presume a 6 percent acidity level. With vinegars, always use the prescribed recipe quantity as a minimum. It is okay to use more to thin a recipe if too thick, but do not use less than prescribed. Recipes too dense can also be thinned with distilled water.

DISTILLED WATER: It is important to have a gallon jug of this water available right along with other canning supplies. Available at most grocery stores, the water has a neutral pH, so it does not affect the acidity of a recipe. Not so with tap water or bottled water. Tap water is artificially made alkaline to protect pipes. This will raise the pH of recipes. One will use distilled water to add to recipes and to perform final pH testing on water bath products; it is used to measure pH on any recipe where oils have a tendency to coat the pH paper, which prevents accurate readings. When this happens, place a tablespoon of product in a half cup of distilled water, mix well, and read. And just a side note here: It does not matter how much distilled water one uses when taking the pH measurement; the reading will be the same with a cup, a quart, or a swimming pool full.

CITRIC ACID: This is canning-specific. It will be found in the canning section of grocery stores or in most establishments selling canning jars. This high-power acid is used in tiny (and I mean tiny) quantities to significantly drop the final pH of a product. This book has few recipes requiring citric acid but suggests using it to lower the pH in others. It is a good product to keep handy if you plan on being a home canner. If a preliminary pH is not to your liking, often a dash of citric acid (a granulated substance) works wonders where the acidifying agent for the recipe might make a final product too liquid. Besides vinegar and citric acid to acidify recipes, use wine and fruit juices like lemon, apple, or orange. When formulating a new recipe, be creative but always test the pH before canning; even better yet, measure as one proceeds and always again 24 hours later.

CANNING SALT: This salt is very different from ordinary table salt. It contains nothing other than sodium chloride. Normal table,salt has anti-caking agents included, and some have iodine, which will turn some canned products purple. Still others like sea salt have many trace minerals, some of which might even rust your product after canning. Use only pure salt or canning salt. Small boxes are available where canning jars are sold. The last chapter gives a big cost-saving suggestion when purchasing salt.

SUGAR: There are several types. Each recipe will specify which type to use: dark brown, light brown, raw, or if nothing is mentioned other than "sugar," it means just plain white, granulated. Some people desire to keep processed or refined sugars out of their canning as much as possible. Honey can be used as a substitute (an expensive substitute) for white sugar in all but jams and jellies, but it is not a one-to-one substitution. For each cup of sugar called for, only add 0.75 to 0.875 cups of honey. Realize also that honey introduces additional liquid into the recipe, so some liquid from some other additive will have to be cooked out before canning or the finished product might be overly liquid. One can also substitute honey for brown sugar. For this substitution, add 2 tablespoons of molasses to each cup of honey used. For me, I'll just stick with the sugar. All these sweeteners have nearly the same initial effects on our bodies, none of them great, although raw honey (not processed) is not only naturally acidic, it is processed within the body as a mild alkaline just like fresh fruits, a big positive that white and brown sugars do not possess. Put another way, honey fights off long-term maladies where other sweeteners like white sugar accelerate their arrival.

HERBS: There is no comparison between fresh and dried, and this is another way home put-up products shine and are classified as incredible. Always use fresh and always put herbs in the pot just before testing the pH. Fresh herbs get their flavors cooked out quickly, so add, test, and can.

Helpful Hints in the Canning Kitchen
Plan Ahead
Know what you are going to do and how you intend to do it. Read through a recipe several times, answering all questions that come up before you begin.

Equipment
It is important to have the correct equipment. One will be working with liquids sometimes much hotter than boiling water, measuring acids, handling glass, and working against time. Proper equipment ensures all goes smoothly and without mishap.

Measuring

Recipe measurements will often be in cups, or a division or multiple of a cup. Below are the various measurements that are derived from the cup.

DRY MEASURE
16 tablespoons = 1 cup
3 teaspoons = 1 tablespoon
2 cups = 1 pint
2 pints = 1 quart
4 quarts = 1 gallon

LIQUID MEASURE
1 cup = 8 fluid ounces
2 tablespoons = 1 fluid ounce
1 pint = 16 fluid ounces
1 quart = 32 fluid ounces
1 gallon = 128 fluid ounces

From these primary measures, one can calculate most called-for kitchen measures. For example, calculate the measure that is sometimes seen: $\frac{1}{3}$ cup. Since 16 tablespoons is not divisible by 3, converting tablespoons to teaspoons (48) and dividing by 3 gives us 16, or 5 tablespoons and 1 teaspoon. We can then calculate $\frac{1}{3}$ cup in the simplest measurement: ($\frac{1}{3}$ cup = $\frac{1}{4}$ cup + 1 tablespoon + 1 teaspoon).

When measuring liquids (not dry measures like sugar or flour), a cup holds 8 ounces. So, 2 tablespoons equals 1 fluid ounce. And for the sake of kitchen measuring, most liquids the consistency of water are equal to a pound per pint. This is not true with honey and other thick liquids.

Common Kitchen Terms

Some common terms are used in this book since everyone has a slightly different idea as to what is meant by specific cutting instructions. This is what is described:

PURÉE: to mash, blend, process, or make smooth (no lumps) by any other means

MINCE: to chop into very fine tiny pieces but not purée

CHOP: to rough-cut into pieces as described: fine (bigger than minced), medium (halfway between fine and large), large (about $\frac{1}{2}$- to $\frac{3}{4}$-inch chunks)

DICE: to cut into squares: small (about $\frac{3}{8}$ inch), medium (about $\frac{1}{2}$ inch), large (about $\frac{5}{8}$ inch).

Turning up the Heat

Sometimes a recipe calling for hot peppers just doesn't have the kick one might desire. There is the option to change the type of pepper, thereby "firing up" a recipe. Heat is a personal choice, and what is too hot for one is not even beginning for another. If a recipe calls for a jalapeño or the optional jalapeño to spice up a recipe, do not add two to make it hotter. This could affect the final pH of the recipe. Instead, if more or less heat is one's desire, use the table below to select a pepper with a heat rating that will make your recipe the level of spiciness you desire.

Peppers are measured on the Scoville Scale—the higher the number, the hotter the pepper. My first book, *Putting Up*, explains how this came to be. Below are some of the more common hot peppers along with their Scoville heat rating.

TYPE PEPPER	SCOVILLE UNITS
Bell	0
Anaheim	1,000–1,500
Jalapeño	2,500–3,500
Serrano	5,000–15,000
Chile	15,000–30,000

Cayenne	30,000–50,000
Thai	50,000–100,000
Scotch Bonnet	100,000–300,000
Habanero	150,000–350,000
Red Habanero	350,000–850,000
Naga Jolokia	850,000–1,000,000
Capsaicin	15,000,000–16,000,000 (sorry, Hotties, not for food—this is the pure chemical used in pepper sprays to ward off attackers)

Pepper Caution

Regardless of which pepper one might select, be certain to wear protective rubber gloves when handling hot peppers. If peppers are touched when gloves are not worn, an act that may be regretted for the following twelve hours, rub hands together with 2 tablespoons of sugar and then wash well with soap and water. Rinse and then coat hands with whole milk for several minutes before rinsing again. Still, if one processes a lot of peppers, plan on feeling the heat from capsaicin, the chemical responsible for hot in hot peppers, for up to twelve hours. And if one does feel heat on hands, be most careful not to rub eyes or touch other sensitive body parts. Best, just wear the gloves.

Preserves—Jams—Jellies

Collectively called jams, these are some of the easiest recipes to produce, but there are some specifics that must be learned, many more than with complex recipes. Each recipe calls for "looking for signs of jelling." Jams will drip off the spatula like water until the pectin begins creating the jelling chains. This is evidenced by elongated drips of slightly slower moving liquid. As seconds pass, this becomes more pronounced. When the last drips have trouble falling from the spatula and actually look like they are jelled, it is getting close to the time to can.

Canning prematurely and jelling may take many hours. The fruit that floats to the top of the jar will need to be shaken over and over again for the duration until final setting up. But there is a fine window when canning jam—if overcooked, the finished product will be rubbery and hard. But even when done correctly, the whole particles will still need to be distributed throughout the jar. After the 2-minute inverted time, each hot jar should be righted and gently shaken to disperse the whole pieces. Keep an eye on the jars and shake every few minutes until jelling locks in place all particulates in the jar.

Putting in the sugar when a recipe calls for standard powdered pectin is straightforward, but when one decides to double the recipe, the sugar must be divided and introduced in two stages. First, half the sugar is poured into the pot during the first rolling boil. The pot is then brought to the first signs of a second boil before the remaining sugar is introduced. This process ensures the temperature of the jam does not drop so low as to prematurely damage the jelling of the product.

I am asked all the time about the quantity of sugar in a recipe and if it can be reduced. You will find the definitive answer on page 54. If you reduce the sugar in your recipe , then you haven't read this important piece of information, which will determine the success of your venture.

pH Testing

Recipes that call for pH testing do so because the recipe is acidified. A first pH test is done just before canning, a time when an incorrect pH level can be adjusted with ease. Canning note #2 (see page 36) gives a suggestion of the initial pH level along with instructions on how to lower to a safe 4.2 threshold. Reading pH paper is easy. Just compare the color of the torn-off strip from the roll with the color chart provided with the roll. On short-range 3.4 to 4.8 paper (only), if it's green, then it's a green-light to process; if it's blue, it can kill you! The only way any recipe in this book will test blue (above 4.5) is if (1) too much of something alkaline was used, like a strong base vegetable; (2) not enough of something acidic was used, like a fruit; or (3) an acidifying agent was left out, was inaccurately

measured, or was an incorrect acid percentage. Still, it must be remembered that fruits and vegetables all have a pH range, so one must ALWAYS TEST.

Temperatures

These are critical measurements in the practice of good, safe canning and should not be taken lightly. The scale for minimum canning temperature versus maximum pH has been calculated to ensure bacteria will not grow in a finished product. If this temperature is exceeded, no additional bacteria are killed but flavors are often diminished. Therefore, canning temperature becomes a critical factor. All temperatures in this text are stated in degrees Fahrenheit, and the canning temperature takes into account the initial cooling effect created by a cold, empty jar.

Canned Ingredients

We have become conditioned to the "tin" flavor that often accompanies some canned products, especially tomatoes. To remove a metallic taste, empty the contents into a small nonreactive pot or skillet and cook on high, stirring constantly at a near boil, for 2 or 3 minutes.

Peeling Fruits

The scald method is quick. With fruit like peaches or tomatoes (at room temperature), cut a small X in the bottom of each before dunking in boiling water for as little time as necessary to loosen the skin, generally under a minute. Remove and plunge into cold water (ice helps). The skins should slide or slough right off. If peaches or similar fruits are not picked when ripe, the process becomes more difficult to impossible. Try again, increasing time in half-minute increments. Ripe-picked fruits are what one wants to be using, so this should not be a problem.

Bay Leaves

Left in the recipe, these crisp leaves pose a potential danger to diners and, thus, should be removed before canning—not always a simple chore. One solution is to count the number of required leaves, place in the smallest saucepan available with a little water, bring to a boil for 10 minutes or hold until the water is half boiled out, whichever is longer. Pour the flavored water into the recipe and either dispose of the leaves or place one in each canning jar as required by the recipe.

the recipes

Preserving is not like cooking. People can attend cooking schools for a year or two and yet only scratch the surface of the art. Not so with canning. Actually, there is nothing complex about canning. A person with zero canning knowledge will emerge after four days from an FDA-sanctioned "Better Process School" knowing more about the science of canning and knowing much safer ways than any grandma who has been putting up jars all her life. The canning primer in this book and its predecessor are based upon the methods taught in those schools.

None of the recipes in this book are complex, and most are produced fairly quickly, especially when one considers he or she is making enough jars for possibly ten or twenty meals. Often, the time required to put up multiple jars, like for a sauce, is not much more than it would take to prepare the same sauce for one dinner. So in a way, canning is also sort of like charging a battery. The time it takes is stored in the little jars to be removed from the pantry when time and place are right to use.

Each recipe has a lead section before ingredients entitled Canning Notes. If the reader has already read the first section of this book (a must-read, not for its literary style but for its canning rules and requirements), she will understand how these notes prepare one to professionally address the recipe.

Canning Notes

1. Type (acid/acidified), Method (hot pack/water bath).
2. pH at time of canning and how to adjust if necessary.
3. Number and size of jars for recipe; alternate jar-size suggestions.*
4. Increase/decrease possibilities for recipe.**

Example:

CANNING NOTES
- **This is an acid hot-pack recipe.**
- **pH is not an issue, so testing is not required.**
- **This recipe makes 8 half-pint jars; jar size should not exceed half pint.**
- **This recipe can be doubled but not halved.**

I have included "multiplied" in many recipes. Making ten times the recipe quantity might be beyond the standard kitchen not to mention pots, but I include this note for those who might be considering a commercial application. Some recipes don't work when multiplied. A simple rule of thumb to remember is that the amount of liquid (water) that needs to steam off while cooking must remain in close ratio with the heated surface area of the vessel and the burner's BTU's (amount of heat generated by the heat source), otherwise the cooking process is slowed and many flavors might change or disappear.

By following the instructions outlined in the first chapter, observing the few guidelines that are included with each recipe, and testing the final product when testing is required, the home-canning experience will be a delightful adventure with splendid rewards.

Jar size is often only a suggestion. Where an 8-ounce jar might get used at one or two sittings, a pint might end up in the refrigerator for a long period. Much depends upon family size. With the family that puts up and boasts a pantry, refrigerators can quickly fill with twenty or thirty partially used jars, so be mindful. Many of us put up in smaller sizes with a few larger ones added to the mix for "big time" occasions. When it comes to preserves, jams, and jellies, an 8-ounce jar is it since there will not be the jelling challenges that pints often experience. Let the notes be the guide.

**Doubling a recipe is easy, dividing a bit more of a challenge as some of the measurements might have to be broken down into smaller measuring units (see page 29).

preserves, jams, and jellies

THOUGH THESE ARE SOME of the easiest recipes to produce, there are some specifics that must be learned—many more than with complex recipes. Each recipe says to "look for signs of jelling." Jams will drip off the spatula like water until the pectin begins creating the jelling chains. This is evidenced by elongated drips of slower moving liquid. As seconds pass, this becomes more pronounced. When the last drips have trouble falling from the spatula and actually look like they are jelled, it is getting close to the time to can.

When products are canned prematurely, jelling may take many hours. The fruit that floats to the top of the jar will need to be dispersed over and over again until finally setting up. But there is a fine window when canning jam; if overcooked, the finished product will be rubbery and hard. However, even when done correctly, the whole pieces of fruit will still need to be distributed throughout the jar. After the 2-minute inverted time, each hot jar should be righted and gently shaken to disperse the whole pieces. Keep an eye on the jars and shake every few minutes until jelling locks everything in place.

Also, putting in the sugar when a recipe calls for standard powdered pectin is straightforward, but when one decides to double the recipe, the sugar must be divided and introduced in two stages. First, half the sugar is poured into the pot. The pot is brought to the first signs of a second boil before the remaining sugar is introduced. This process ensures the temperature of the jam does not drop so low as to prematurely begin jelling the product, thus damaging it.

There are other spreads in this category that are not for breakfast as well as some breakfast spreads that are well worth bringing out for other meals. Sweet for meat is a newer sensation. It is a good one, and I dwell on it throughout this volume. Peaches and pork form a union, chicken and raspberries a partnership, duck and orange a marriage. I have experienced apricot jam on flounder, cactus-pear jam with rattlesnake, and onion pepper jelly on burgers. Then there is a goodly assortment ready to work as toppings for the likes of ice cream and cheesecake. If there is only one chapter from which you decide to specialize, make it this one.

are preserves, jams, and
jellies different?

There is a difference, although slight, between the three products.

PRESERVES utilize the intact whole fruit or, with large fruits such as peaches, small chunks of whole fruit. These succulent bits are especially savored and make preserves a favorite, but they are more time-consuming to produce since the fruit has a tendency to float to the top of the jar after canning. So, until the jelling process locks the pieces in position, the maker is kept busy monitoring and periodically shaking jars long after the process should be complete.

JAMS are close enough to preserves to be a twin, just not an identical one. They are smoother because the fruits are finely mashed, ground, or chopped, providing a more even distribution of fruit in the finished product.

JELLIES are only a distant cousin to jams and preserves, just as jams are a twin to preserves. Fruit jellies are made like jams, but the juice is separated from the fruit so only the richly flavored liquid makes it to the jar. The translucent jelly has the taste and color of the fruit, but it has none of the fruit.

Regardless of which is made, there is a major difference between store-bought and home-preserved. The secret lies in the quality of the fruit. The home canner has the ability to pick or purchase just-picked, vine-ripened produce from local farmers. There is no equal to this advantage.

lemon-cherry jell

Cherries, like their early blossoms, release a subtle bouquet of flavors, while the lemon offsets the immense sweetness of this jell by giving it a tart tang. With the taste of sweet and sour, this makes a most versatile preserve.

CANNING NOTES

- This is an acid hot-pack recipe.
- pH is not an issue, so testing is not required.
- This recipe makes 8 half-pint jars; jar size should not exceed half pint.
- This recipe can be doubled but not halved.

INGREDIENTS

2 lemons, thinly sliced, seeded but not peeled, each slice quartered

1 cup water

2½ pounds ripe red or yellow cherries, pitted and medium-chopped (for a clear jell, use finely chopped dried cherries)

6 cups sugar

1 pack liquid pectin

DIRECTIONS

Place prepared lemon in a nonreactive pot with the water; bring to a boil, reduce heat, and simmer for 5 minutes. Add cherries and sugar. Bring to a rolling boil, add pectin, and bring to a second boil. Time for 3 minutes, but begin checking for signs of jelling halfway through.

When ready, hot-pack into sterilized jars, seal, and invert for 2 minutes only. (When making jam, it is important to not let the jam jar sit upside down for MORE than two minutes! When the jars are first inverted, the fruit will imme-diately congregate at the surface. As the jelling process begins, each time the jars are turned, the fruit's ascent to the surface will slow. Watch carefully; when movement has slowed suf-ficiently, shake the jars to distribute the fruit uniformly. Check again after a few minutes to see if shaking again is necessary. If the jars are not filled prematurely, the fruit sets within 5 or so minutes.)

SERVING SUGGESTIONS

Lemon cherry jell is one of those special put-up recipes that reaches beyond the breakfast table. It works well as a morning marmalade but makes an excellent addition on top of roast fowl such as chicken, duck, or pheasant. It also plays a nice duet with pork or ham, and removes much of the gaminess from wild venison and boar. It does not stop at the main course or the hunter's table. Red cherries, yellow lemon rind, and tinted glaze turn a "plain vanilla" scoop of ice cream into something closer to art, pleasing to both sight and palate.

fruit marmalade

Not everyone is a marmalade fan, but for those who are, and this includes Ian Fleming's James Bond, there is no comparison between store-bought and homemade—especially when made with tree-ripened fruit. And even if fruit must be purchased from a grocery store (meaning it is rarely tree-ripened), when competing against the best commercial brands, you will ALWAYS take home the blue ribbon. Why, you ask? It's simple. Industry brings out the worst. Every manufacturer is competing for your dollar, so price, fancy labels, and pretty jars are foremost in the marketing mind. He has to advertise, pay his employees, pay his rent, and, don't forget, make a profit; his distributor requires a profit; and the retailer often demands more than all the others combined. Guess how this comes together to work? Cheap ingredients!

CANNING NOTES
- **This is an acid hot-pack recipe.**
- **pH is not an issue, so testing is not required.**
- **This recipe makes 14 half-pint jars; pints can be used but jelling will be slow.**
- **This recipe can be halved but not doubled.**

INGREDIENTS
8 cups fruit (lemon, orange, grapefruit,*
  individually or in combination)
3 cups water
2 packs pectin
11 cups sugar, divided

DIRECTIONS
Thinly slice and seed the lemons and/or oranges. For the grapefruit (if used), the membranes between the plugs are tough and must be removed. Peel off the outer skin of the fruit, reserving only half. Cut each grapefruit in half and then cut between each plug and around the outer perimeter; spoon out the plugs and put aside after measuring. Cut any excess white pith from the reserved skins and slice into strips approximately $1/16$ x $1/4$ to $1/2$ inch.**

Place the lemons, oranges, and grapefruit rind in the canning pot; add the water and bring to a boil. Reduce heat and simmer for 10 minutes.

Add the grapefruit plugs (if used) and pectin, and turn heat to high. Bring to a rolling boil, holding for 1 minute before adding half of the sugar. Bring to the beginning of a second boil before adding the remaining sugar. Bring to a fierce rolling boil and begin timing for 2 minutes. Check for signs of jelling after the first minute.

Once proper jelling is assured, remove from heat and quickly ladle into sterilized jars, making sure each gets a fair share of each fruit. Seal and invert for 2 minutes only. When jars are placed upright, gently shake the jars periodically until jelling sets the pieces of fruit.

SERVING SUGGESTIONS
It goes without saying that marmalade on toast or English muffins is a morning delight. But marmalade hardly stops at breakfast! When chicken is baked, broiled, fried, or rotisseried, then slathered with a top-quality marmalade, the simplest and least expensive of birds is turned into one of those meals a family will demand again and again. The same goes for pork chops. Stir a teaspoon of crushed red pepper flakes into a half cup of jam just to fire up the taste. Use your imagination. Whatever pairs well with sweet will work well with marmalade. Try it on flounder!

*Limes can be added or substituted; however, lime rind is really tough and must be removed and cooked with baking soda as described below for 20 minutes. A lime-grapefruit marmalade makes a pleasant yet unique spread as well as a world-class addition to many a mild white fish.

**To avoid the toughness of the rind, peel all the fruit with a peeler and reserve the rind after removing any remaining white pulp. Cut the strings of rind into short strips and dump some or all into a pot with 2 cups of water and 1/8 teaspoon of baking soda. Bring to a boil, reduce to a simmer, and cook for 10 minutes (if using lime, see further directions above). Rinse and drain well. If it is the bitterness of the rind you want to avoid, peel and discard the rind; but when cutting the slices of fruit, leave the sections larger, for they will break down during the cooking process.

orange-fig marmalade

For the thousand years before commercial enterprises began turning out bleached white sugar, families used honey to sweeten their food. Back then, many lived on farms and society was agrarian. The honey used was a by-product of a farm denizen as necessary as the mule—the bee. These were maintained to pollinate crops, the wax from the hives was turned into candles for light, and, lastly, the nearly forgotten honey was used as a sweetener. The Civil War in our country was a clash between two societies, agrarian and industrial, a sort of honey versus white sugar. White sugar won, but remember, honey has a long-range positive effect on our bodies that other sweeteners do not.

The delicate flavors of yellow figs and the lasting freshness of oranges combine to make a great presentation, while the recipe provides a bit of nostalgia as we remember, through our taste buds and our genes, families sitting around farm tables having breakfast, eating fresh home-baked breads with home-churned butter and homemade preserves spread on top.

CANNING NOTES

- This is an acid hot-pack recipe.
- pH testing is not required.
- This recipe makes 6 half-pint jars; half-pint and pint jars are best suited for this recipe.
- This recipe can be halved only.

INGREDIENTS

6 cups stemmed and quartered figs
2 cups water
2 thin-skinned oranges, sliced, seeded, and slices quartered
2 lemons, sliced, seeded, and slices quartered
4 cups honey
2 packs liquid pectin

DIRECTIONS

Place the figs in a canning pot with the water, bring to a boil, and simmer for 10 minutes.

Add the citrus fruits and the honey. Bring all to a rolling boil. Add the pectin, return to a boil, and, after 1 minute, begin checking for signs of jelling. Jams made with honey never jell like jams with sugar but, still, signs will show.

When ready, ladle into sterile jars, seal, and invert for 2 minutes only.

SERVING SUGGESTIONS

Fig jam is a very popular breakfast spread. As a marmalade, it will be the star of the morning table; as an hors d'oeuvre over Brie, it is a party stopper; and for cooking, use on pork tenderloin, pork chops, and chicken after coming off the heat source.

red tomato jam / red tomato marmalade / red tomato conserve

When we think preserves, we think fruit. So, yes, these three recipes are right on target. The tomato might be more commonly considered a vegetable, but, in fact, it is a fruit or, more specifically, a berry. It is the highest pH fruit and creates the division between fruits and vegetables. It is only fitting then that we make a preserve. Like all fruits, tomatoes are sweetest when picked blood-red ripe. So this becomes the standing prerequisite for great jam, no exceptions.

Unlike the seeds in many berries like blackberries, tomato seeds lend bitterness to the finished spread, so it is best to remove as many as you can. Excessive juice means longer cooking times, which equates to reduced flavor. So after peeling (by scalding in boiling water for 1 minute, page 35), core and halve the tomatoes by cutting through their "equators," not their "poles." This exposes the five or so seed cavities. Squeeze out the juice and most of seeds will flush with it. A finger in each crevice will chase out any recalcitrant cling-on seeds. End result—no bitter taste, cooking time is shortened so flavors are enhanced, and jelling will occur much faster.

red tomato jam

CANNING NOTES
- **This is an acid hot-pack recipe.**
- **pH is not an issue, so testing is not required.**
- **This recipe makes 10 half-pint jars; half pints are best suited for this recipe.**
- **This recipe can be halved only.**

INGREDIENTS
8 cups tomatoes, peeled, cored, juiced, seeded, and chopped medium (about 5 pounds)
2 lemons, seeded and chopped fine, or ¼ cup lemon juice
2 packs pectin
1 teaspoon allspice
10 cinnamon sticks
½ tablespoon butter (optional)
8 cups sugar

DIRECTIONS
Cook prepared tomatoes at a slow boil in a non-reactive canning pot for 20 minutes.

Measure out 6 cups of the finished tomatoes and discard the remainder. Add the measured tomatoes to the pot plus all remaining ingredients except the sugar and bring to a strong boil.

Add the sugar and return to a rolling boil that cannot be stirred down. Remove the cinnamon sticks and place 1 in each canning jar. Time the boil for 1 to 1½ minutes, keeping an eye out for good jelling signals.

Pour into sterile jars, seal, and invert for 2 minutes only.

red tomato marmalade

CANNING NOTES

- This is an acid hot-pack recipe.
- pH is not an issue, so testing is not required.
- This recipe makes 10 half-pint jars, which are best suited for this recipe.
- This recipe can be halved but not doubled.

INGREDIENTS

7 cups peeled, halved, squeezed, seeded, and chopped tomatoes

1 orange, peeled, sliced, seeded, and slices quartered

1 lemon, peeled, sliced, seeded, and slices quartered

1/2 teaspoon cinnamon

1/2 teaspoon allspice

2 teaspoons lemon zest (optional)*

2 teaspoons orange zest (optional)*

2 packs pectin

1 tablespoon butter

12 cups sugar, divided

DIRECTIONS

Place tomato chunks in a pot over medium heat and simmer for 15 minutes, stirring continuously.

Add remaining ingredients except sugar, turn heat to high, and continue to stir. When a rolling boil begins that can no longer be stirred down, add half the sugar. As boiling begins for a second time, add the remaining sugar and, stirring constantly, return to a full boil. Continue stirring while timing for 2 minutes. Check for strong jelling signs after 1 1/2 minutes.

When jelling is assured, remove from heat. Pour into sterile jars, seal, and invert for 2 minutes only.

Some folks love rind while others abhor the bitterness. Any marmalade aficionado will add the rind.

red tomato conserve

CANNING NOTES
- **This is an acid hot-pack recipe.**
- **pH is not an issue, so testing is not required.**
- **This recipe makes 8 half-pint jars, which are best suited for this recipe.**
- **This recipe can be halved but not doubled.**

INGREDIENTS
6 cups peeled, cored, juiced, seeded, and chopped medium tomatoes
2 cups fresh blueberries, errant stems removed
¼ cup freshly squeezed lemon juice
2 packs pectin
½ tablespoon butter (optional)
8 cups sugar

DIRECTIONS
Place tomato chunks in a pot. Over low heat, simmer for 10 minutes, stirring continuously.

Add remaining ingredients except sugar and continue to stir. When a rolling boil begins that can no longer be stirred down, add the sugar. Stirring constantly, return to a full boil. Continue stirring while timing for 2 minutes. Check for strong jelling signs after 1½ minutes.

When jelling is assured, remove from heat. Pour in sterile jars, seal, and invert for 2 minutes only.

SERVING SUGGESTIONS
It goes without saying that these three contenders will find their way onto many a breakfast table. But breakfast is only a first daily performance for this trio. I like to serve good food in a presentation that is pleasing to the eye, especially if I can also avoid being a slave to the preparation. If I can enjoy art for dinner, I'll do it, especially if there is no extra mile.

One of my favorite summer salads is a simple layered spread of ripe tomato slices topped with sliced medallions of mozzarella cheese and basil leaves on top, all aligned across a plate with the discs overlapping by half the length of the plate. Spill a small puddle of quality olive oil above the top starting point and drizzle balsamic vinegar into the center. Repeat this at the end of the tomato line but below. When all is fresh, this is a truly divine and refreshing dish—so much so that I hate to have to wait all winter to enjoy it. In comes tomato jam or marmalade! Winter tomatoes never have that bright red look of summer tomatoes nor do they have much taste, so I supercharge the same salad by spooning a line of the preserves or marmalade along the center. The sweet taste of fresh tomatoes returns and the salad becomes a year-round enjoyment.

Another great suggestion—use the tomato preserves on a sandwich! A tomato slice on a chicken salad sandwich made in the morning for lunch at the office turns even the best breads into soggy paste after four hours of capillary action. But, with lettuce below and tomato preserves instead of the tomato above, the sandwich bread remains as it was when sliced—a perfect sandwich.

As with many of these recipes in this book, the limit is one's imagination. There are no big red circles with a diagonal red line intimating "Not for use on chicken, etc."

rainbow pepper jelly

Green bells have twice the vitamin C of a tree-ripened orange, and red bells have four times. All peppers start out green; but the varieties that continue on to other colors are not picked green, because they will command a higher price later even though they will perish sooner. They are also sweeter than green. As pepper season arrives, all bells plummet in price, making these put-up delectables a most reasonable canning opportunity. Pepper jellies have arrived, front and center, and are a mainstay of home entertaining. The reason is obvious, the hors d'oeuvre is prepared quickly and is always appreciated. The problem with store-bought jellies is that they lack in taste, but the simplest home-prepared jelly explodes with flavor. This is another chance to shine as a home canner.

CANNING NOTES
- This is an acidified, sugar-saturated, hot-pack recipe.
- pH is not an issue, so testing is not required.
- This recipe makes 12 half-pint jars; half pints are best suited for this recipe.
- This recipe can be halved but not doubled.

INGREDIENTS
1 cup seeded and deveined, medium-diced green bell pepper*

1 cup seeded and deveined, medium-diced red bell pepper

1 cup seeded and deveined, medium-diced orange bell pepper

1 cup seeded and deveined, medium-diced yellow bell pepper

1 cup seeded and deveined, medium-diced purple bell pepper

3 cups white vinegar (distilled)

2 tablespoons red pepper flakes

13 cups sugar

1 tablespoon butter

2 packs liquid pectin

DIRECTIONS
Place all ingredients except the pectin in a non-reactive pot. Bring to a rolling boil for 1 minute. Add the pectin and, when the second rolling boil commences, begin a 2- to 3-minute count. After 1 minute, begin checking for signs of jelling. (It is important not to can pepper jelly prematurely or, even if canned in the a.m., you will be shaking jars well into the night. It is equally important not to overcook or the finished jelly will be tough and rubbery.)

When just right, ladle into sterile jars, seal, and invert for 2 minutes only.

SERVING SUGGESTIONS
Pepper jellies have been served at gatherings for the better part of the twentieth century. Spooned over cream cheese, there remains little that is faster to prepare. I have tried them all, and water crackers are by far the best accompaniment for this hors d'oeuvre. But this colorful jelly can be used very successfully as a topper to cooked white fish, chicken, and pork. Or add a spoonful to a burger and watch smiles break out.

*If heat is desired, reduce the green bell pepper by half and add ½ cup green jalapeños.

blackberry-lemon marmalade

The season of berries is an exciting time. There is nothing quite like the flavor of freshly picked ripe berries. Every region has its wonders. In coastal Maine, it's the tiny wild blueberries. In the Northwest, blackberries are definitely world-class. When I lived in Seattle, my yard was fenced because of a pool, and the fence was surrounded by bramble. I was considering clearing it all out when I noticed big black buds on the stickers. I investigated, picked, ate, and then pigged out. By season's end, I looked like I'd spent a week chasing Brer Rabbit through the briar patch. So sweet are freshly picked ripe blackberries that the addition of lemon adds just enough tartness to give an exciting and complementary flavor to one of my favorite fruits. We introduced this recipe at a farmers market one July. It has been in high demand ever since.

CANNING NOTES

- **This is an acid hot-pack recipe.**
- **pH is not an issue, so testing is not required.**
- **This recipe makes 14 half-pint jars; half pints are best suited for this recipe.**
- **This recipe can be halved but not doubled.**

INGREDIENTS

8 cups blackberries, rinsed and partially crushed
**3 lemons, seeded and chopped into pea-size
  chunks**
2 packs pectin
1 tablespoon butter
13 cups sugar, divided

DIRECTIONS

Place the blackberries and lemons in a non-reactive pot with the pectin and butter, and bring to a strong boil. Add half the sugar. When the mixture shows further signs of beginning a second boil, add the remaining sugar and bring to a fierce rolling boil. Begin timing for 2 minutes and then watch for signs of jelling. Depending on the water content in the berries, jelling signs may take longer.

When ready, ladle into sterile jars, seal, and invert for 2 minutes only.

SERVING SUGGESTIONS

This is a breakfast delight. Because I have so many diverse canned items, and because I enjoy this marmalade in the morning, I seldom use it elsewhere. However, I once tried dumping a whole jar over a big wedge of Brie at a fundraiser. I was surprised to see the crowd that gathered around my little black-and-white offering while forsaking more traditional canapés. Coming home that night, I opened another jar and painted it on a skinless chicken breast as it came off the grill. It was then I knew I'd be running out of blackberry marmalade long before any berries were again ripe for picking.

blueberry marmalade

In my neck of the woods, fresh blueberries herald the summer like strawberries announce the spring. But it matters little when these tiny sweet berries come of age; when they do, a season changes for the better and so does our health, because blueberries are a super antioxidant. My first book offers the basic preserve while this book has the more complex marmalade. Every pantry should contain some of both.

CANNING NOTES
- **This is an acid hot-pack recipe.**
- **pH is not an issue, so testing is not required.**
- **This recipe makes 12 half-pint jars, which are best suited for this recipe.**
- **This recipe can be halved but not doubled.**

INGREDIENTS
5 cups blueberries, partially crushed
3 thin-skinned oranges, stem ends cut off, seeded, and roughly chopped*
2 lemons, stem ends removed, seeded, and roughly chopped*
2 packs pectin
1 tablespoon butter
11 cups sugar, divided

DIRECTIONS
Place the fruit, pectin, and butter into a non-reactive pot over high heat. Stir often while bringing to a substantial rolling boil. Hold for 1 minute before adding half the sugar. Return to a boil and add the remaining sugar. When a rolling boil commences a second time, begin a 2-minute count. Check for signs of jelling. It may take another minute, depending upon the water in the berries. When ready, pour into sterilized containers, seal, and invert for 2 minutes only.

Cut the fruit into slices so each can be adequately seeded and then run through a processor to chop into large chunks, or slice, seed, and quarter the slices.

SERVING SUGGESTIONS
Of course this is a breakfast delicacy. There is nothing quite like fresh blueberry marmalade on an English muffin, crumpet, or just plain old toast, although many are beginning to admit specialty breads like Ezekiel have raised the bar. But this spread does not have to be stashed once breakfast is history, for it works well over vanilla ice cream too. My favorite usage, along with a plethora of other homemade preserves, is to fold the marmalade within an omelet along with a small block of cream cheese. Want to get fancy? The French might call this *oeuf au confiture*. My granddaughter, Ashley, calls it a cream-cheese-and-jelly omelet, and it always guarantees a return visit.

prickly pear cactus jelly

My introduction to this unusual delight came when I was visiting the Grand Canyon. The enormity and natural beauty was so magnificent that I burst into tears at my first glimpse. I have traveled all over the world, but nothing got to me quite like our natural wonder. A few nights later in a restaurant in Flagstaff, Arizona, I had a rattlesnake appetizer with cactus pear jelly. Wow, I began to wonder if Arizona had it all: the Grand Canyon, cactus, rattlesnakes, and wonderful residents.

CANNING NOTES
- **This is an acid hot-pack recipe.**
- **pH is not an issue, so testing is not required.**
- **This recipe makes 5 half-pint jars; half pints are best suited for this recipe.**
- **This recipe can be doubled but not halved.**

INGREDIENTS
3 cups prickly pear juice*
¼ cup freshly squeezed lime juice
4 cups sugar
1 pack liquid pectin

DIRECTIONS
Add all ingredients except the pectin to the canning pot and bring to a strong boil. Add the pectin and return to a rolling boil. Time for 1½ minutes. Watching for jelling signs after 1 minute.

When ready, pour into sterile jars, seal, and invert for 2 minutes only.

*6 cups of the cactus fruit makes about 3 cups of juice. Wash and scrub the fruit, taking care not to get skewered by the spines. These will soften during cooking and will be strained off later. Quarter the fruit and place in a pot with just enough water to cover. Mash the quartered fruit with a potato masher, bring to a boil, reduce heat, and simmer for 30 minutes. Strain with a fine sieve or several layers of cheesecloth. Measure 3 cups and discard any remainder.

SERVING SUGGESTIONS
Once again it is the sweet and meat combination. Rattlesnake meat, both bone in and boneless, is available online; but the cost, beginning at nearly $60 a pound, is prohibitive. Best leave that one to regional cuisine. Still, the jelly is unique, wonderful tasting, great on morning breads, and, since rattlesnake tastes like chicken . . . well, you get the idea.

too much **sugar?**

I am asked all the time about the quantities of sugar in a recipe and if they can be reduced. The answer is "no" when using standard pectin. In order for jelling to take place, the brix level (sugar measure = sugar in fruit + sugar) of the mixture must be between 55 and 60. Below this level, pectin is ineffective and jelling will not occur. The amount of sugar in each recipe is based upon an average brix measurement for the fruit(s) being used. One can get sophisticated and purchase a brix meter for a more exact measurement of brix levels.

mango preserves

It is rare that one finds mango preserves for sale. It is no wonder, the large bulk fruit has a thick skin and a big pit resembling a cuttlefish bone one finds in a canary cage. Of all the fruits, mango to me is the most luscious. On our tiny sailboat, coasting south along Central America, my son and I would spyglass the distant shoreline, looking for mango and coconut trees. It was always worth the effort to anchor beyond the breaking surf and swim ashore to gather nature's fallen wild bounty. In Panama, we often wondered why local children so full of energy didn't climb the trees to get the fruit. They just stared, hoping for fruit to fall. Little did we know that one does not climb the mango. The first time I sent my son up one of these trees, he threw down fruit to ecstatic but mouth-agape kids. It was shortly thereafter that we learned of the miserable side effect of climbing the mango tree. It is a member of the sumac family and, like poison ivy, can leave a climber miserable for a time.

CANNING NOTES
- **This is an acid hot-pack recipe.**
- **pH is not an issue, so testing is not required.**
- **This recipe makes 8 half-pint jars; half pints are best suited for this recipe.**
- **This recipe can be doubled but not halved.**

INGREDIENTS
6 cups peeled and seeded, small-chopped mango*
  (about 6 pounds whole fruit)
¼ cup freshly squeezed lime juice
6 cups sugar
½ tablespoon vanilla
1 pack liquid pectin

DIRECTIONS
Place the prepared fruit in a nonreactive pot with the lime juice, sugar, and vanilla. Bring to a rolling boil before adding the liquid pectin. Bring to a second boil and time for 2 minutes (3 if recipe is doubled), and then watch for signs of jelling.

   When ready, pour into sterilized jars, seal, and invert for 2 minutes only.

There is a stringy fiber within mango pulp, and this is the reason for chopping it into small thumb-nail pieces.

SERVING SUGGESTIONS
Like all preserves, this goes well with breakfast. The mango is a tropical fruit and therefore makes a marvelous complement to more exotic tropical or Caribbean meals. For example, trigger fish fillets coming off the grill with a dollop of mango preserves alongside each plate is island heaven. Try it—I guarantee when the plates are collected, there'll not be a drop of preserve or fish on any plate. As a steamy summer supper or as a luncheon salad, cold-cook red snapper cubes in a ceviche (or citrus) marinade and finish each plate by placing a tablespoon of the preserve on top of the serving. Never a negative comment will be heard, just plenty of kudos.

red cherry preserves

There was a time many years ago when I vividly recall driving in our family convertible through the Yakima Valley in Washington State, gorging on just-picked cherries bought from roadside stands while giggling kids in the backseat spat pits straight up to catch the airstream above. These were fun adventures in the simplest of times, often the best of life. Fresh cherry preserves are a delight, both as a breakfast spread and as a condiment for all things pig, fowl, and fish. I never fail to make two double runs of this preserve and yet always run out even before cherry blossoms herald the coming of spring.

CANNING NOTES
- **This is an acid hot-pack recipe.**
- **pH testing is not required.**
- **Recipe makes 8 half-pint jars; half pints are best-suited for this recipe.**
- **This recipe can be doubled but not halved.**

INGREDIENTS
5 cups pitted and chopped cherries*
  (Bing or equivalent), about 4½ pounds
¼ cup freshly squeezed lemon juice
5 cups sugar
½ tablespoon butter
1 pack pectin

DIRECTIONS
Place the fruit in a pot with all but the pectin and bring to a rolling boil. Add the pectin and return to a rolling boil. Begin a 2-minute time count and watch for jelling after 1 minute.

When ready, pour into sterile jars, seal, and invert for 2 minutes only.

*Cherry juice stains! So, when you begin the task of pitting fruit, wear old clothes and have a damp cloth ready to mop up spilt juice. The chore goes quickly. Using just your fingers, break open the cherry and squeeze out the pit. When juice spits out, quickly wipe down the backstop, wall, or cabinet. Later, put Clorox in the water to clean your counters and fingers as you sterilize the jars.

SERVING SUGGESTIONS
The cherry preserve stash in the pantry will work well for any meal. The deep red of cherry preserves goes so well against the anemic white of oven-cooked pork and fowl that I often cannot help but add a dollop to brighten up the plate.

apple conserve

Fall is apple time. I often wonder if the third quadrant of our calendar was not named for the action of apples in September! Or could it be that Newton named the season?

Sinfully delicious, apples are truly one of God's gifts to mankind. And yet only a handful of us recall the story of Johnny Appleseed. By the time he got to the West, apple trees were flourishing nationwide. Apples grow in many states and many climates, and boxes of them find their way to grocers all across our land in all seasons because the fruit stores so well. If you are blessed with a tree or live in a region where apple trees flourish, take advantage. If not, don't be disheartened—as with Eve, a great apple is always within reach.

A conserve is like a jam or preserve but with added fruits and flavors to make it complex. The complex flavors of this recipe are perfect for a crispy autumn morning breakfast biscuit or toast, but on a pork chop, it is like a coronation crowning.

CANNING NOTES
- **This is an acid hot-pack recipe.**
- **pH testing is not required.**
- **This recipe makes 7 half-pint jars; half pints are best suited for this recipe.**
- **This recipe can be doubled but not halved.**

INGREDIENTS
5 cups peeled, cored, and chopped red tart apples, like Winesaps (about 7 pounds)
1 cup water
2 thin-skinned lemons, thinly sliced, seeded, and slices quartered
1/2 cup chopped dried cherries
1/2 cup chopped nuts (almonds, pecans, walnuts, cashews, etc.)
1 pack pectin
6 cups sugar

DIRECTIONS
Place all ingredients except the sugar in a non-reactive pot. Bring to a rolling boil, add sugar, and return to a rolling boil before beginning a 2-minute count. Watch for jelling signs after 1 minute.

When proper jelling is assured, pour into sterile jars, seal, and invert for 2 minutes only.

SERVING SUGGESTIONS
I like to usher in each new month and season with new recipes I have just put away. For my granddaughter, it is a way of saying not only has a new month arrived, but also new and exciting recipes await her developing little palate. I make a lot of preserves, so I decided I'd try this one with a new medium. I warmed some of the conserve until soft and then poured it over apple fritters. As with ancients honoring a harvest, the apple took center stage. Another presentation is to put a tablespoon of conserve over a scoop of vanilla ice cream. Surprise everyone at the table, but be prepared to be asked for several additional spoonfuls before each scoop is gone. And lest we forget the preamble, one will never view a pork chop in quite the same light again.

apple butter

The term *butter* is derived from the way a product spreads—not what is in the mix. Unlike jams and jellies prepared in kitchens, six or eight jars at a time, the harvesting of apples is celebrated with a preparation of butter. Whole apples are cooked down in huge copper cauldrons while being stirred with a wooden paddle fit for canoeing. Slowly cooked for long periods (eight hours or more) and using the skins and cores to provide the necessary pectin, apple butter contains little sugar by comparison to sauce or jam. Apples can be added and mixed and matched for quantity, added sweetness, bitterness, and flavor. Likewise, just before canning, a portion of the butter could be made into a conserve by using either dried or acid ingredients only, like fruit (but no more than a cup per single recipe) to be safe.

Although this recipe can be multiplied into the hundreds of pounds without increasing the surface area of the pot and the BTU's of heat, the breakdown of the apples could take much longer, maybe days. Two suggestions: use a bigger pot, maybe twice as big when making a double run, or make two single runs simultaneously.

CANNING NOTES

- **This is an acid hot-pack recipe.**
- **pH testing is not required.**
- **This recipe makes 8 half-pint jars; half pints are best-suited for this recipe.**
- **This recipe can be doubled or multiplied but not halved (see caveat on page 37).**

DIRECTIONS

Cook apples in juice for 20 to 30 minutes until soft, mushy, and coming apart.

Press thru a strainer, food mill, or sieve, leaving behind stems, cores, seeds, and skins. Add strained sauce to a pot with sugar or honey, bring to a boil, and reduce heat. Stir periodically on low; stir more frequently on medium low; and stir nearly constantly on medium, knowing that the job will get done much faster.

When the butter is thick, ladle into sterile jars, seal, and invert for 2 minutes only.

INGREDIENTS

6 pounds apples, mixed but none overly sweet, quartered

1½ cups apple juice, freshly pressed or juiced (not pasteurized)

3 cups sugar (brown is optional but is richer and changes the flavor), or 2½ cups honey

SERVING SUGGESTIONS

Use like preserves. Apple is a wonderful addition to all things pork, and I am not the first one to discover this. I've been seeing roasted whole pigs with apples stuffed in their mouths my entire life. When serving a roast pork dish like tenderloin or chops, place a ramekin with about 2 ounces of apple butter in the center of each plate just for dipping. Simple, easy to fix, and healthy—the kids will thank you for it. So will grown-ups!

persimmon jelly

Persimmon was at one time far more common a tree than we see today. The reason? It's kin to ebony, an extremely hard, fine-grained wood that was used to make the heads of golf clubs (woods or long-range drivers). The near fate of the persimmon tree is not alone. Can you believe the giant redwoods were nearly almost all converted into cigar boxes! My, how we can be a thoughtless nation of excesses sometimes.

I love to watch young people bite into a ripe persimmon for the first time. The look of fear over trying something new gives way to exploration after they bite through the waxy astringent skin and the first sweet juices, unlike anything they might have ever tasted, hits the palate and blossoms in their mouth. You just know they are thinking, "I need to get a lot of these." Too bad they are so expensive. Ripe fruit perishes rapidly, so persimmons must be picked unripe for commercial markets. This can be a turnoff. Then there is the feel of the meat on the palate. Peaches might have their fuzz, but persimmons have this strange waxy alkaline feel on the tongue and cheeks, and the interior has a slimy texture—all challenges when made into preserves, so this is an ideal candidate for a jelly, something I rarely do.

CANNING NOTES

- **This is an acid hot-pack recipe.**
- **pH testing is not required.**
- **This recipe makes 4+ half-pint jars; half pints are best suited for this recipe.**
- **This recipe can be doubled but not halved.**

INGREDIENTS

4+ pounds ripe persimmons, blossoms removed and fruit quartered
2¼ cups water
3 tablespoons freshly squeezed lime juice
1¼ cups honey
1 pouch liquid pectin

DIRECTIONS

Place fruit in a nonreactive pot. Add water and bring mixture to a boil. Mash the persimmons with a potato masher, reduce heat, and simmer 15 minutes. Remove from heat.

Press pulp through a strainer to remove pits, and then measure 3½ cups juice. Discard any remainder. Stir in the lime juice and honey (heated honey pours better and leaves less behind). Bring mixture to a rolling boil. Add the pectin and return to a rolling boil for 2 minutes before beginning jell testing.

When signs of jelling are assured, pour into sterile jars, seal, and invert for 2 minutes.

SERVING SUGGESTIONS

I don't want to insult anyone's intelligence here. We all know what to do with jelly! But just the same, I am one who gets bored quickly with the spread on toast or English muffin routine, and I have a pantry stuffed full of jars to use on meat, fish, and fowl. So let's say we try something outside the standard cooking envelope as an added benefit. Because the jelly is without fruit chunks and is opaque, it can be used invisibly to subtly yet uniquely flavor without an overpowering tour de force. One such way is to add persimmon jelly to homemade chili. Recall my discussions on sweet and meat.

onion-pepper jelly

There is a pepper jelly for every occasion: plain bell pepper, hot pepper, garlic pepper, pepper-specific like jalapeño or habanero pepper, and even multi-pepper like seven-pepper jelly. There are endless combinations, but all contain three common ingredients: vinegar, sugar, and clear liquid pectin. Many of these creations come in pretty colors, and I am often asked if I have green or red pepper jelly, to which I always respond with a resounding "NO!" simply because I detest chemicals, and colored pepper jellies are dyed with food coloring (some colors have recently been determined unsafe).

This onion pepper jelly has a little of both red and green bell peppers to give it color as well as depth of taste, but there is a predominately and commanding onion flavor with the sweet, making it an hors d'oeuvre general as well as a cooking condiment colonel.

CANNING NOTES

- This is an acidified, sugar-saturated, hot-pack recipe.
- pH testing is not required.
- This recipe makes 7+ half-pint jars; half pints are best-suited for this recipe.
- This recipe can be doubled but not halved.

INGREDIENTS

1½ cups medium-diced red onion
½ cup medium-diced red bell pepper
½ cup medium-diced green bell pepper, or ½ cup seeded and finely chopped jalapeños
6½ cups sugar
1½ cups distilled vinegar
½ tablespoon butter
1 pouch liquid pectin

DIRECTIONS

Prepare the onion and peppers and place in a nonreactive pot with the sugar, vinegar, and butter. Bring to a rapid rolling boil. Add the pectin and return to a rolling boil before beginning a 1½-minute count. Check for signs of adequate jelling after 1 minute.

When ready, pour into sterile canning jars, seal, and invert for 2 minutes only.

SERVING SUGGESTIONS

If the cheese is the thing with which we'll catch the interest of the king (just to twist the great bard's words), then the cheese to use might be English Stilton. However, one can always use cream cheese. Spoon this jelly over a favorite cheese and serve with water crackers for a showstopping hors d'oeuvre. For cooking, the usual suspects are chicken, pork, and even cuts of red meat work; but go outside the box by experimenting with a giant portabella mushroom steak. Paint the tops and bottoms of each mushroom with olive oil, place top down in a 425-degree oven, and bake for 18 minutes. Remove, sprinkle the inside well with cheddar cheese, and add a small amount of minced purple onion on top along with green and red bell pepper stripes. Return to the oven just long enough for cheese to melt, remove, and place a tablespoon of onion-pepper jelly in the center to complete your masterpiece.

sweet onion jam

Not all jams belong on the breakfast table. This is one that does not. Sweet onions differ from their eye-watering, breath-tainting cousins in that they hold more water and consequently less of a sulfuric smell. When I lived in Seattle, there was always a Walla Walla Sweet somewhere to be had. Other locales have theirs, with Maui producing maybe the sweetest and Vidalia (through marketing) producing one of the best known. But in California, it's the Sweet Imperial; in Arizona, the Grandex; in New Mexico, the Nu Mex Sweet; and in Texas, a big, big onion called Tex Sweet. The Spanish Sweet is not so sweet; though great for preparing other dishes while not crying over the prep, don't use them for this recipe because they're just not sweet enough.

It's fun to be unique, especially when one delivers something unusual and yet extraordinary. So it will be with sweet onion jam. Easy to make and with a plethora of uses, this simple, iron-rich, put-up delectable will add a new kind of excitement to hamburger and steak dinners.

CANNING NOTES
- **This is an acidified hot-pack recipe.**
- **pH will be below 4. To reduce, add additional vinegar in small amounts.**
- **This recipe makes 3+ half-pint jars, half pints are best-suited for this recipe.**
- **This recipe can be doubled, but read prep instructions first.**

INGREDIENTS
¼ cup butter
3 tablespoons olive oil
4 pounds sweet onions, thinly sliced, and slices quartered
1 cup sugar (raw or white)
½ cup dark brown sugar
½ cup balsamic vinegar
¼ cup dark red wine
½ teaspoon salt

DIRECTIONS
In a large skillet (I use a huge cast-iron fry pan and yet still have to do the onions in two portions), melt the butter with the olive oil; when hot, add the onions. Stirring frequently, sauté onions on medium-high heat until they begin to brown and caramelize. When ready, set aside.

In a nonreactive pot—not a cast-iron skillet—add the remaining ingredients and bring to a boil, then reduce heat to medium before adding the onions. Continue to cook until mixture begins to thicken.

Ensure pH is below 4.3 before ladling onion jam into sterilized jars, topping off with extra liquid if necessary to ensure solids are covered before sealing. Invert for required 2 minutes.

SERVING SUGGESTIONS
I have yet to serve this onion jam as a side or on top of steak without a big smile coming from dining company. The jam is equally good with chicken or lamb, and on burgers. As an hors d'oeuvre, poured over goat cheese and served with water crackers, the strange onion concoction makes the better known classic pepper jelly over cream cheese seem like it belongs on Maslov's lowest tier as basic subsistence.

— relishes —

NO PANTRY IS CONSIDERED well stocked that does not contain a few relishes. We all have heard of hot dog relish and hamburger relish, but few know about those same products with fresh flavor. Homemade makes it a different world. When I canned my first jar of relish after purchasing commercially made "store bought" for forty years, I had the distinct feeling that I'd been duped all those years. More recently, a friend of mine bought me a VERY expensive jar of relish as a gift. The label was of a quality hardly ever seen, and the jar was as fancy as a jar can get, with the lid embossed with the company logo. The performance was furthered with a fancy name, but as soon as I saw corn syrup and dried onions, I knew the relish would have little flavor. I knew the main ingredients were not harvested fresh and ripe during peak season. The expensive jar might have made a grand paperweight, but it was going to be worthless as a relish. I opened it anyway. The $16 jar of relish tasted like a 5-cent debacle.

It seems there is a relish to augment just about anything and everything one is willing to improve upon. In the South, green tomato relish was a staple on the table whenever rice and chicken, two former boring and bland partners, were served. A black-eyed pea relish, colloquially called Texas Caviar, was the approach to similar dishes in the West, while in the upper Midwest, corn relish graced tables with pork or potatoes. In the arid Southwest, cactus fruit condiments ruled.

There is nothing quite as extraordinary as mustard greens or turnip greens with a dollop of homemade northeastern piccalilli on top, or an after-Thanksgiving turkey sandwich smothered with cranberry-orange relish. These are the little special treats that turn a year of ordinary into exquisite with just an hour or two of quiet morning canning and a twist of a lid when the time is right. Enjoy these relishes and make a bunch. Over the coming year, you'll use enough to wish you had made more!

caponata

This recipe's origins are from the island of Sicily. Like so much of the melting pot that is our nation, our foods reflect the diasporas of those peoples—poor, humble, and yearning to be free. The vast empire that once was Rome has not only left its mark on our government, law, and language, the former cohorts' families have cooked up some of the most prolific foods now residing in the United States; consider pizza and spaghetti. Caponata might not soon be the exception. Although maybe eleven hundred years separate the last Roman chariot race with the first serving of this relish, consider that Sicily is, to a large degree, isolated from the lines of commerce linking Italy with the rest of the European continent; consequently, caponata just might be a purer representation of the glory that was Rome. Once you taste it, you'll agree!

CANNING NOTES

- **This is an acidified hot pack recipe.**
- **Initial pH will be under 4.2; to reduce pH, add additional vinegar.**
- **This recipe makes 12 pint jars; pints and half pints work best.**
- **This recipe can be halved, doubled, multiplied.**

INGREDIENTS

3 pounds very ripe tomatoes, peeled, seeded, juiced, and chopped
1 cup olive oil, divided
6 cups medium-chopped onion
6 cups celery, cut into ¼- to ½-inch chunks
3 pounds eggplant, skins on, cut into ¾-inch cubes
4 cups chopped olives (with pimentos, if desired)
12 ounces capers
4 cups cider vinegar
2 cups sugar

DIRECTIONS

Sauté the tomatoes until soft with ¼ cup olive oil.

Place the remaining oil in a canning pot with the onion and sauté until clear. Add the celery and eggplant; stirring frequently, continue until the eggplant is soft. Add the remaining ingredients and bring to a canning temperature of 195 degrees.

Check pH before filling sterile jars. Seal and invert for specified 2-minute period.

SERVING SUGGESTIONS

Traditionally, caponata is served as an antipasto. Spread on toast points, it is a great and easy way to begin a meal. My two favorite uses for this relish are for breakfast and supper:

1. For breakfast, prepare a two-egg omelet. As the egg begins to firm, add 2 tablespoons of freshly grated Parmesan cheese spread about. Add 2 tablespoons of warmed caponata on top of the cheese before folding the omelet.

2. For supper, split a loaf of Italian or French bread. Paint the insides with olive oil and crushed garlic. Place the bread under the broiler to warm. Layer both sides with sliced rounds of mozzarella cheese, return to the broiler to allow the cheese to soften. Remove from the oven, and ladle on hot caponata. This will become one of those simple meatless suppers that is remembered and requested.

apricot and lime relish

This relish is reminiscent of summer and its flavors. The flavor of apricot is bolder than peach, and often this smaller fruit is forgotten because of huge commercial peach crops. It is ideal as an addition to lighter fare like those enjoyed on hot summer evenings, such as white fish or grilled chicken. The relish works equally well on heavier meats like lamb, alleviating some of the heaviness with the lightness of the fruits. But no matter how one uses the relish, you will feel faint summer breezes while dining, even if it's snowing outside.

CANNING NOTES
- **This is an acidified hot-pack recipe.**
- **pH should be under 4, but a pH up to 4.2 is okay; to decrease, add more vinegar.**
- **This recipe makes 4 or 5 pint jars; consider making pints and half pints.**
- **This recipe can be halved, doubled, or multiplied.**

INGREDIENTS
6 cups chopped apricots
2 cups medium-diced bell pepper (red, green, or combination)
2 cups medium-diced red onion
4 limes, peeled, sliced, seeded, and slices halved
2 cups distilled vinegar
2 teaspoons salt
1½ cups honey
¼ cup finely chopped, tightly packed cilantro

DIRECTIONS
Place all of the ingredients except the honey and cilantro in a nonreactive canning pot and bring to a canning temperature of 200 degrees F. Add the honey and cilantro, and stir in well before checking pH.

Ladle relish into sterile jars, seal, and invert for 2 minutes minimum.

SERVING SUGGESTIONS
Drizzle the relish generously on a piece of grilled white fish just after it emerges from the grill, allowing the flesh to draw in the flavors as it finishes. Pass on the baked potatoes, selecting instead a nice baguette. From start to sitting down, gourmet dining is underway in less than fifteen minutes.

Imagination is a remarkable thing. The ability to marry many flavors in a harmony of taste, like using diverse instruments in an orchestra, is not the purview of foodies and chefs alone. Anyone with a thought of what might work should give it a try. I give no guidance when I hand out trial jars, because it helps to keep the receivers' minds working outside what might become their limitations. The feedback is often amazing. After taste-testing this relish, my mother used it as a topping on a lamb burger, while a friend made an hors d'oeuvre using Melba rounds spread with goat cheese and topped with it. Both of these suggestions were excellent, and every canner of this relish should try them. Used as above or simply as a centerpiece of a salad, this summer relish has many untold uses.

fig relish

Often the simplest of recipes can produce the finest of dishes. This is one such relish. It is simple to make and inexpensive when figs are gathered in season, and the sealed jars on the shelf stand ready throughout the year for when needed. Figs are a most delicate fruit, so it is only fitting that this relish be utilized on or with delicate fare. Roll the multifarious flavors of the recipe across the tongue of your imagination and consider what you might do. I frequently open a jar, so I quadruple the recipe. Some of the many uses follow below.

CANNING NOTES
- This is an acidified hot-pack recipe.
- pH will be below 4; if above 4.2, add more vinegar.
- This recipe makes about 7 half pints; jar size is not critical.
- This recipe can be halved, doubled, or multiplied.

INGREDIENTS
1 cup minced shallots
1 teaspoon salt
¾ cup balsamic vinegar
2 cups honey
4 pounds ripe figs, chopped
¼ cup finely chopped fresh mint
1½ teaspoons chopped fresh rosemary

DIRECTIONS
Place the shallots in the bottom of a nonreactive canning pot; sprinkle with the salt and allow to rest for 10 minutes. Add the vinegar, turn on the heat, and simmer for 5 minutes before adding the honey and the figs.

Turn the heat to medium high and bring the temperature to 190 degrees. Stirring often to prevent burning, maintain the 190-degree temperature for 5 minutes or until relish begins to thicken. Add the herbs, stirring in well to distribute flavors throughout.

Test pH, hot-pack in sterile jars, seal, and invert for 2 minutes minimum.

SERVING SUGGESTIONS
This relish begs to partner with chicken. Grilled chicken, baked chicken, or store-bought rotisserie chicken (for when you just can't see yourself cooking) with a dollop of fig relish ladled over or as a side turns just plain old chicken into something to write about. Since this is not the heavy dinner of steak and potatoes, select light accompanying partners to form a well-balanced meal. For the vegetable, try a nice salad or steamed fresh string beans. And for that quick energy boost we get from carbohydrates (but still keeping light in mind), consider corn either on or off the cob, depending on the formality of the meal.

peach relish

Summer relishes, delicate and often subtle like the season's breezes, are delightful complements to light suppers, especially in the heat. But sometimes one still desires lightness when summer has passed. The problem is that those delicious fresh tastes are not always so easy to find. There is nothing that says summer quite like the peach, and this peach relish might best remind us of those "lazy, hazy, crazy days of summer."

There is a two-part requirement for the relish to be successful. The first is to pick ripe or purchase ripe local harvest. This ensures that our sun has done the job of ripening that cannot be accomplished commercially with time on trains or trucks or with gases. The second is to be mindful not to exceed the suggested canning temperature. The minimum required canning temperature ensures no bacteria will grow, but with each degree over, flavors diminish. These are the putting-up secrets to successfully capture those summer tastes later in the year.

CANNING NOTES
- This is an acidified hot-pack recipe.
- Initial pH will be below 4; for pH over 4.2, reduce with vinegar.
- This recipe makes 9 half-pint jars; jar size does not matter.
- This recipe can be halved, doubled, or multiplied.

INGREDIENTS
6 cups finely diced peeled peaches
2 cups medium-diced red bell pepper
1 cup medium-diced green bell pepper
1 cup medium-diced red onion
1 cup sliced and quartered peeled cucumber
1 cup honey
¼ cup minced garlic
1½ cups cider vinegar mixed with ¼ cup tomato purée, or 1¼ cups balsamic vinegar
½ cup finely chopped hot pepper of choice (seeded and deveined is optional)
½ cup finely chopped, tightly packed mint (leaves with tender stems only)

DIRECTIONS
Place all but the mint in a nonreactive pot and bring to 187–190 degrees F. Add the mint and stir in well; check pH while holding the heat.

Working fast, immediately fill and seal sterile jars while pot is maintained at temperature. Invert jars for 2 minutes minimum.

SERVING SUGGESTIONS
This relish belongs on top of a piece of light, grilled, broiled, or baked white fish like grouper, flounder, stripper, tilapia, mountain trout, or one of our inland lakes fish. Light is the key—not fishy or oily like mackerel or cod. Fowl and pork, although not as light, work great as well. Again, it is imagination that makes and limits its use. With a complementary light vegetable and a simple whole grain baguette, this becomes a complete meal in less than twenty minutes. It's even easier and lighter in a nice salad: On a bed of butter lettuce, add a selected grouping of mixed baby greens and an ice cream scoop full of peach relish; dressing is optional. A salad lunch with a pint jar of peach relish will serve four in under a minute!

sweet and spicy corn relish

As an early teen summering on a working farm, I often remember that all children would be summoned to pick corn as supper approached. Holding hands we would skip to the barn, harness a mule to a cabbage cart, and gleefully head to a nearby cornfield. Four of us would pick from the back of the cart as Johnny edged the animal onward. Heading home on the dirt roads and sitting cross-legged on the cart, we'd shuck the fifty or more ears to feed a table of sixteen. The corn would go straight from the cart into pots of boiling salted water. I was spoiled for life, and corn never tasted quite that good again. Now you can lock in those splendid fresh flavors for a continuing treat throughout the year. I love this recipe, and use it a lot, so much so that I put up enough to dedicate an entire pantry shelf in its honor.

CANNING NOTES

- This is an acidified hot-pack recipe.
- The pH will be below 4; if above 4.2, vinegar acidity was incorrect—start again.
- This recipe makes six pint jars; pints and half pints are best suited.
- This recipe can be halved, doubled, or multiplied.

INGREDIENTS

3 cups cider vinegar, divided
2 teaspoons Colman's Dry Mustard
2 teaspoons turmeric

1½ cups sugar, or 1 cup honey
¾ cup freshly squeezed lime juice
¼ cup red pepper flakes
1½ teaspoons whole celery seed
1 teaspoon pure salt
1½ cups medium-diced red bell pepper
1½ cups medium-diced green bell pepper
2 cups medium-diced red onion
3 cups sliced celery (stalks sliced lengthwise once and cut every ¼ inch)
18 ears (approximately) corn, cut (not scraped) off the cob (9 cups total)*

DIRECTIONS

Make a paste with a little of the vinegar, dry mustard, and turmeric. This way the powders will diffuse easily without clumping in the pickling solution.

In a nonreactive pot, add the remaining vinegar, sugar, lime juice, pepper flakes, celery seed, and salt. Bring to a boil and add the mustard/turmeric paste. Stir in well. Add all remaining ingredients except the corn and bring to a boil. Add the corn, return to a boil, reduce heat, and simmer for 5 minutes.

Check for safe pH. Return to just under a boil (205 degrees F) and prepare to can. Ladle relish into sterile jars and top off if necessary with pickling solution from the pot, ensuring vegetables are covered. Seal and invert for the required 2-minute period.

To cut fresh corn off the cob, hold a sharp knife at a 20-degree angle to the cob and slice in until hitting the cob. Then, with the blade tilted slightly inward, very carefully cut down the cob. You'll know if you cut into the cob because they are tough. Just reduce the angle of the blade and continue.

SERVING SUGGESTIONS

Corn relish makes a remarkable addition to a simple green salad. Aside from bringing many diverse flavors and a touch of heat and sweetness to the greens, it adds a glorious bouquet of sprinkled colors: reds, purples, greens, and yellows against a backdrop of green. With a simple cider vinegar and olive oil dressing, there is neither a healthier nor a tastier salad combination.

But corn relish isn't just for salads. Whenever there is rice on one of my plates, a scoop of corn relish replaces the former obligatory block of butter. Unless using another put-up recipe, consider opening a jar when serving chicken, fried, grilled, or baked. A served plate might look like this: chicken, broccoli or spinach, and maybe brown rice as a carbohydrate, each taking up a third of the plate. A little 3-tablespoon mound of relish in the center does wonders for the bland starch, livens up the green vegetable, and is scrumptious with the chicken. The bright colors add a carnival-like atmosphere to the plate, a feature fine chefs charge extra to achieve.

And there is a medicinal advantage. It was not so long ago that a condiment bowl of pickled offerings like this corn relish was a staple of dining tables. There was a reason and, like many old rooted traditions, 5,000 years of human history is seldom wrong. Cider vinegar is a remarkable health aid. John Adams (1735–1826) refused to accept the position as ambassador to France until his government guaranteed that he'd have a supply of homemade cider vinegar. Its benefits are impressive.

cranberry-orange relish

Even before winter begins to knock on our doors, but just about the same time trick-or-treaters do, the New England and Northwest coast cranberry fields are in full harvest. The season of these berries may be short-lived, but the flavor speaks autumn itself, and no Thanksgiving table is complete without something cranberry. My first book, *Putting Up,* featured Cranberry Chutney, and before the holiday seasons commence, this has always been one of my biggest sellers at the farmers market. But I have always wanted something a bit less overpowering than chutney, something subtle yet with the taste of cranberry, maybe with fruity accents and the lightness of a relish. What I created was equally good with a just-carved steaming turkey and much better than anything yet tried on those leftover turkey sandwiches. Last Thanksgiving season, when both products were sampled, this relish outsold the chutney three to one.

CANNING NOTES
- This is an acidic hot-pack recipe.
- pH is not an issue; no pH testing is required.
- This recipe makes 6 half-pint jars; jar size is not critical.
- This recipe can be divided, doubled, or multiplied.

INGREDIENTS
5 cups fresh cranberries, washed, picked through, and roughly chopped
2 oranges with zest but no pith, seeded, sliced, and chopped
¾ cup apple juice/cider
2 cups sugar
½ cup finely chopped sweet onion
2 tablespoons minced fresh garlic
¼ cup+ minced crystallized ginger

DIRECTIONS
Place all ingredients in a nonreactive pot. Bring to just under boiling, stirring often to prevent burning.

Reduce heat and ladle into prepared jars, seal with sterile lids, and invert for the required 2-minute minimum.

SERVING SUGGESTIONS
It doesn't take Thanksgiving to enjoy or fully appreciate cranberry-orange relish. When I was creating this recipe, I went through several store-bought rotisserie chickens until I got the flavors just as I wanted them; I'd slice off a big chunk of breast meat and smother the relish on top; third try was a charm, as they say.

For an hors d'oeuvre in the autumn, I spill half of a small jar of relish over a block of cream cheese and surround it with water crackers. Quick and easy as well as colorful, it never fails to draw the crowd. Also, a party favorite is a paste of either chicken or turkey chopped and mixed with equal parts of relish. Place on toast points as an exquisite canapé that will set apart a hostess.

hot pepper relish

I left this recipe in the relish section rather than moving it to All Things Hot, simply because it is up to the maker to decide how hot the hot will be. Much like the sweet pepper relish from my first book, *Putting Up* (but with the addition of a Scoville increment determining the heat level to best serve a home canner's needs), these jars quickly become family favorites and are standing favorites of farmers market patrons. We produce three heat scales, one for each tolerance: mild yet warm, medium but getting there, and screaming hot for those who dare. Interestingly, it is the hot that vanishes first.

Not so ten years ago! Back then, six mild jars might have lasted the summer without a taker. "The times they are a changin'." Bob Dylan, you were correct!

CANNING NOTES

- **This is an acidified hot-pack recipe.**
- **pH will be below 4.2; to lower, add 2 tablespoons each of vinegar and sugar.**
- **This recipe makes 7 half pints; pints and half pints are best suited.**
- **This recipe can be halved, doubled, or multiplied.**

INGREDIENTS

6 cups medium-diced bell peppers, assorted colors
2 cups medium-chopped yellow onion
1 cup cider vinegar
1 cup sugar
½ tablespoon salt
½ tablespoon mustard seeds
Jalapeños, chiles, and/or habanero peppers, to taste:
  Very Mild: ¼ cup finely chopped jalapeño, seeded and deveined
  Standard Mild: ¼ cup finely chopped jalapeño, seeds and veins left in
  Medium: ¼ cup finely chopped chile peppers
  Hot: ¼ to ½ cup finely chopped habanero peppers (seeds in or out)
  Screaming Hot: 1 cup finely chopped habanero, but reduce bell peppers by ½ cup

DIRECTIONS

Place the prepared vegetables in a canning pot with the vinegar and bring to a boil. Take pot off the heat, allow temperature to drop below 200 degrees F, and then test pH. If at or below guidelines, continue. If not, drain vinegar and use another measured cupful per single recipe.

Add remaining ingredients and bring to a canning temperature of 205 degrees F.

Check pH again, ladle into sterile jars, seal, and invert for 2 minutes minimum.

SERVING SUGGESTIONS

This is a simple relish with a bit or a lot of zing. It works well, just like store-bought, but the flavors are so fresh and rich in comparison that where the store varieties find their way, sometimes reluctantly, to hotdogs and burgers, this relish will be heaped on and also used to enhance many supper plates featuring animal, fish, fowl, and vegetarian main courses. Further, by using a medley of different colored peppers, the color-enhanced plate of food is delightful art. A favorite is to ladle over pan-fried, broiled, or baked freshly caught white-meat fish like bass.

— chutneys —

CHUTNEYS ARE SOME of the most enjoyable recipes to preserve. For one, they are sweet, a majority have that cursed tooth, but more importantly, chutneys have a plethora of uses. There is hardly a meal or occasion where one cannot find a use for chutney. Sweet lowers heat. In its native India, 400 years before refrigeration, chutney was created to offset the hot of curry and other spices used to preserve meats. In the simplest translation, chutney (*chut nai*) means "to taste good"; a more meaningful translation might be "to make edible." Early sea captains sailing the trade routes—from India around the Cape of Good Hope, up the coast of Africa, and across the Atlantic to the New World's fledgling colonies—brought these recipes made with unheard of fruits. Befuddled colonists substituted what was then growing. Today, chutneys abound in America, are more popular than ever, and have taken on a mystic quality of their own.

Often referred to as the fastest hors d'oeuvre in America, these sweet yet often spicy condiments can be ladled over many different cheeses (Brie and cream cheese being the most widely used) for a party treat that will cause crowding around the table. Specific chutneys are great with pork, fish, and fowl; are used to enlighten certain starches like rice or potatoes; and with curry dishes, of course, they go together like a horse and carriage. On the following pages are enough chutneys for many different applications. Select the ones that best suit your lifestyle. There are more than enough for everyone.

mango chutney

It could have been Major Grey who, in the early 1800s, started the occidental love affair with mango chutney; but, alas, he is the stuff of legend. However, the legend continues.

Today, chutney is more popular than ever, and mango is the crown jewel of fruits for chutney. Since the colonial introduction in this country, chutneys have added a depth to dining that meat and potatoes just couldn't fathom.

This recipe uses mango as the predominate fruit, as found in the original chutney, and is the perfect foil for curry dishes. The sweet offsets the heat in curry powder, while the mango complements meats in the sauce. I made a dozen jars and offered them at a Saturday farmers market. My peach chutney had always been a favorite, but the mango marched away like the soldiers ordered off to war by the old Major Grey—gone in a flash, the peach was left behind to do KP!

CANNING NOTES
- **This is an acidified hot-pack recipe.**
- **pH will be low. If above 4.2, add additional vinegar.**
- **This recipe makes 16 half-pint jars; pint jars work equally well.**
- **This recipe can be halved, doubled, or multiplied.**

INGREDIENTS
8 cups peeled, seeded, and roughly chopped (thumbnail-size chunks) mango (about 12 pounds)

2½ cups sugar
1½ cups finely diced red onion
1 cup raisins
1 cup finely chopped crystallized ginger
1 cup cider vinegar
½ cup finely chopped hot peppers (seeded and deveined is optional)
¼ cup freshly squeezed lime juice
¼ cup red pepper flakes
1 tablespoon salt
2 teaspoons minced garlic
½ teaspoon turmeric

DIRECTIONS
Place all ingredients in a nonreactive canning pot. Stirring often to prevent burning, bring to a temperature of 195–200 degrees F; continue cooking, allowing chutney to thicken to the consistency of thin pancake batter. Pour into sterile jars, seal, and invert for the required 2-minute minimum.

SERVING SUGGESTIONS
To serve mango chutney with a curry dish is like a homecoming reunion for the two, but many serve it over cream cheese as an hors d'oeuvre. Try ladling it over English Stilton, just to remember the British and the part they played in securing such a delectable as chutney from their far-flung colonies. On a simple water cracker, the two stars will make a third star of the hostess. The mango flavor always reminds me of exotic warm days with cool breezes and times of leisure, so I use this chutney accordingly. A tablespoon dropped on a conch salad, on a trigger fish ceviche salad, or as a side to coconut-encrusted shrimp never fails to bring compliments.

orange and date chutney

Where once there was one, now there are a thousand chutneys, many created for a specific pairing. Today, in the hands of creative persons, new ways continue to explode. Although oranges and dates might appear at first to be strange bedfellows, the two grew near each other in biblical times, which speaks volumes, and this might well be a rendition or even reinvention of a pairing many thousands of years old. Finding real citrus fruit chutney is like a treasure discovery. The delicate flavors don't lend themselves to big commercial batches, so there are only a few. Keep this in mind as you serve it. One could find himself pressed into small-batch processing.

CANNING NOTES

- This is an acidified, sugar-saturated, hot-pack recipe.
- pH is low and is not a concern; no testing is necessary.
- This recipe makes 10 half-pint jars; half pints and pints are best.
- This recipe can be halved, doubled, or multiplied.

INGREDIENTS

6 cups white vinegar
2 cups light brown sugar
3 cups white sugar
1 to 2 tablespoons crushed red pepper flakes
2 cups finely chopped red onion
4 cups peeled, seeded, and chopped oranges
¾ to 1 pound golden raisins
3 cups pitted and chopped dates
2 teaspoons salt
½ cup orange zest

DIRECTIONS

Pour the vinegar into a canning pot and bring to a boil before adding the sugars and the crushed red pepper. Stir well until the sugars are completely dissolved, reduce heat slightly, and add the onion; cook until clear. Add all but the zest and cook on medium until the chutney begins to thicken, about ½ hour. Bring temperature up to 190 degrees F; add the zest and mix well. Pour into sterile jars, seal, and invert for 2 minutes minimum.

SERVING SUGGESTIONS

Chutney over a cheese always makes for a delicious party treat. To be unique and get away from the cream cheese syndrome, the orange would pair exceptionally well with Camembert. Going fancy, one might try this chutney with duck. Reading through this volume, duck and orange are a natural, so duck with a sweet orange chutney would be over the top. On a simpler note, a more common fowl like Cornish game hens or just plain chicken will pair equally well.

blueberry chutney

Chutneys can be to a dinner plate what pillows are to a bed. The latter just isn't as comfortable without the former. And once again, it's the sweet and meat thing. Commercially, chutneys are seldom produced. Because of extended cooking times, equipment gets tied up for excessive periods when two or three quicker products might otherwise be completed. It all comes down to money. And as is often the case, the trick to making good chutney is in the slow cooking, rendering from the fruits and vegetables their natural flavors and sugars. Blueberries, a super antioxidant, are a favorite fruit and, although they stain everything from clothing to teeth, I cannot imagine a cupboard much less a world without them.

CANNING NOTES

- **This is an acidified hot-pack recipe.**
- **Because of the low alkaline content, no pH testing is necessary.**
- **This recipe makes 7 half-pint jars; jar size is irrelevant.**
- **This recipe can be halved, doubled, or multiplied.**

INGREDIENTS

½ **cup cider vinegar**
½ **cup balsamic vinegar**
½ **cup freshly squeezed orange juice**
1½ **cups light brown sugar**
1½ **cups finely chopped sweet onion**
6 **cups fresh blueberries**
¾ **cup golden raisins**
¼ **cup whole yellow mustard seeds**
¼ **cup minced crystallized ginger**
2 **tablespoons orange zest**
1 **tablespoon red pepper flakes**
½ **tablespoon allspice**
½ **tablespoon vanilla extract**

DIRECTIONS

Put the vinegars, orange juice, sugar, and onion in a nonreactive canning pot. Cook over medium heat until onion is clear, about 5 minutes. Add the remaining ingredients, turn heat to high, bring to a boil, reduce, and cook down until blueberries begin to break down and chutney just begins to thicken. (Blueberries contain enough pectin to jell on their own, so do not overcook; otherwise, you'll get jellied chutney!)

Bring temperature to 190 degrees F. Ladle into sterile jars, seal, and invert for 2 minutes minimum.

SERVING SUGGESTIONS

All the usual suspects work here, cream cheese, Brie, and even white cheddar. Over or beside wild or domestic fowl, this chutney can do the trick; the same goes with pork. The deep bluish purple always adds to the look of a plated supper.

Here is something a bit different. Make a mixture of one part blueberry chutney with two parts yogurt to make a dressing for a luncheon salad. If yogurt is not your thing, try mixing equal measures of chutney and mayonnaise (homemade being best). For the salad green, use a lettuce like romaine, add a few strips of ham, smoked turkey, bacon (if you dare), and some diced chicken—one, some, or all of the above. A sliced hard-boiled egg goes well, as does some grated white cheddar. Once the salad is to your liking, pour on the dressing and enjoy an unforgettable yet light repast.

kiwi fruit chutney

The fruit is not from New Zealand as one might expect (being named for the country's national bird) nor is it from neighboring Australia (although the first commercially grown crop among Occidentals was in that country). The fruit is native to China. Harvested for over a century now in English-speaking countries, the benefits of this unique fruit are still being discovered as medical science compiles more about the needs and demands of the human body. Since the early 1970s, kiwis have been grown in the United States, and many regions harvest a crop today. The fruit is mild and light-tasting, producing a chutney that is the same yet filled with exotic and unique flavoring.

CANNING NOTES
- **This is an acidified hot-pack recipe.**
- **Because acidified pH will be low, a cursory test will be fine.**
- **This recipe makes 8 half-pint jars; half and whole pints serve this recipe best.**
- **This recipe can be halved, doubled, or multiplied.**

INGREDIENTS
6 cups coarse-chopped peeled kiwi
2 cups medium-chopped yellow onion
2 cups sugar
1½ cups distilled vinegar
⅓ cup raisins
⅓ cup golden raisins
¼ cup minced garlic
3 tablespoons peeled, minced or grated fresh ginger
2 teaspoons mustard seeds
1 teaspoon cayenne pepper
½ teaspoon coarsely ground pepper
½ teaspoon salt

DIRECTIONS
Place all ingredients in a canning pot and bring to a canning temperature of 190 degrees F. Ladle into sterile jars, seal, and invert for 2 minutes minimum.

SERVING SUGGESTIONS
This is one of the few chutneys that should not be poured over cheese, but it is the chutney that should often accompany chicken salads or chicken salad sandwiches. As a fancy yet simple appetizer, whip up a simple chicken salad, place a slice of kiwi on a round cracker, top with a mound of the salad and then a dollop of chutney. This chutney makes a delightful accompaniment to fish or chicken, as it does also to a most healthy plate of protein-rich beans and rice.

cherry chutney

With cherry season, there comes a feeling of jingoism. I don't know whether it is because of Washington's alleged cherry tree mishap or images of the nation's capitol when the cherry blossoms are in full bloom, but when I see the first farmer's roadside stands touting just-picked cherries, my chest swells and I am once again a 125 percent United States citizen. Pitting cherries is a chore, and mess abounds as the juices spray and stain. The fruit is tart but the flavor extraordinary, and the color of certain varieties is a deep red—all benefits, so it's time well spent. Maybe just make one day "Cherry Day," with preserves and chutney done for the year. For the rest of cherry season, one can enjoy eating the succulent little orbs while lounging in the hammock, thinking about what comes next.

CANNING NOTES

- **This is an acidified hot-pack recipe.**
- **Because of high acid levels, only a cursory pH test is necessary.**
- **This recipe makes 6 half-pint jars; half and full pints are best suited.**
- **This recipe can be doubled or multiplied but is not easily halved.**

INGREDIENTS

4 cups stemmed and pitted sweet red cherries*
1 cup medium-chopped white onion
1 cup cider vinegar
1 cup honey
1 cup golden raisins
¼ cup grated orange peel
¼ cup crystallized ginger
½ tablespoon ground cinnamon
1 teaspoon cayenne pepper
½ teaspoon salt
½ teaspoon allspice

DIRECTIONS

Place all ingredients in a canning pot over medium-high heat; stirring often, cook down until signs of thickening show. It should not be runny, but remember that cooling will further thicken a finished product.

Fill sterile jars, seal, and invert for 2 minutes minimum.

Pinch or squeeze the fruit and the pit will pop out; use both hands and the job is done in no time.

SERVING SUGGESTIONS

Cherries and duck are a close second to orange and duck, so when the desire for that rich dinner builds, consider using the birds minus their legs and thighs for duck a l'orange, reserving the latter for duck confit with cherry chutney. Recipes for confit abound online. Served on a bed of greens with 2 or 3 tablespoons of cherry chutney as a side along with a French baguette, this becomes a most fitting continental excursion. These rich and somewhat expensive meals become a pleasant treat every once in a while and remind us of just how good homemade can be and how much money is not being spent dining out.

Back to reality, cherry chutney and cream cheese are a natural, but spread over goat cheese, it gets gourmet. Pork is another option; serve with cherry chutney to complement a simple chop, or to infuse a tenderloin, or turn the pork into a confit just like duck. The only challenge is rounding up the necessary fat. About this time, one might be wondering if this author is trying to kill the readership. French cooking is often heavy and fatty yet delightful; the French lifespan is 2½ years longer than the average American's, and the French population is leaner. Is it their incessant smoking, their fatty foods, their red wines? Something here doesn't tally. Enjoy confit!

eggplant chutney

Eggplant chutney has no fruit, so cooking time is greatly reduced, although preparation time steals a bit of this advantage. It is one of the most expensive recipes in this book to make because of the balsamic vinegar, yet it is well worth the effort and the cost! The nearly black finish, with red chunks of dried tomato, the purples of various eggplants, plus the colors of the peppers and squash, is striking even before the flavor hits one's taste buds. Make enough to give a few jars away at gifting times. It's unique and always makes an extra special present. It won't be forgotten.

When our company was in full production, we made over ninety mouthwatering products, yet a version of this chutney was the only product to make it across the Atlantic to be sold in one of London's most famous boutiques. I often consider this a favorite, like if I had to "get out of Dodge" right now with only one jar in my saddlebags, this would be it. Why? It's so yummy that its uses could fill this book!

CANNING NOTES

- This is an acidified hot-pack recipe.
- Initial pH should be below 4.3; add more vinegar ¼ cup at a time to drive pH lower; if chutney is overly liquid, add ¼ teaspoon citric acid at a time until pH is safe.
- This recipe makes 7 to 9 pint jars; jar size does not matter.
- This recipe can be doubled or multiplied but not easily halved.

INGREDIENTS

½ pound each Chinese and Japanese eggplant (skin intact), cut into ½-inch cubes; or 1 pound eggplant (skin intact), cut into ¾-inch cubes*
¾ pound red bell pepper, large-diced
¾ pound yellow bell pepper, large-diced
½ pound yellow squash, cut into ½-inch cubes
½ pound zucchini, cut into ½-inch cubes
½ pound red onion, diced
½ pound sun-dried tomatoes, medium-chopped
¾ cup sliced jalapeños
1 tablespoon minced garlic
2 tablespoons tightly packed fresh thyme
1½ tablespoons tightly packed fresh oregano
2 tablespoons tightly packed fresh basil
1 tablespoon coarsely ground pepper
½ cup extra virgin olive oil
2 pounds light brown sugar
4 cups balsamic vinegar

DIRECTIONS

Combine all ingredients in a nonreactive pot, place on high heat, and bring mixture to 205 degrees F, stirring often to prevent burning while allowing to thicken.

After taking an initial pH test and adjusting if necessary, hot-pack in sterile jars, seal, and invert for 2 minutes minimum.

The oriental varieties of eggplant have lighter skins and denser flesh, making a more colorful display and a firmer chutney.

SERVING SUGGESTIONS

Let's put it this way, it's tough to imagine what this chutney might not be good on! I love putting a big black glob next to chicken and then watching an unsuspecting table guest stare at it, wondering if it is tar, before mustering the courage to taste it. One taste later, she demands to know where I bought the stuff. It's fun to smile and whisper, "I made it—it's simple." On white fish (from flounder and tilapia to trout or catfish), it adds a symphony of flavors, often giving a whole different perspective to "fish for dinner." Spooned over St. Andre cheese with a surround of water crackers, eggplant chutney will be the hors d'oeuvre hit. And, just to round off eating, try spreading on luncheon sandwiches or stuffing a tablespoon or two into pita pockets to complement the likes of chicken or tuna salad. You can also serve as a side with pork or any curried dish. This chutney is "the must" for every well-stocked pantry and the "gotta give" when gifting friends.

seafood chutney

My first experience with fish and sweet sauces was at Ivar's in Seattle. That was many years ago, but Mr. Haglund's baked salmon slathered with a simple preserve still lingers on the taste buds of my memory. When I arrived in Charleston, South Carolina, after a grueling 15,000-mile sailing voyage, where my son and I ate fish EVERY day, a friend Joanne treated me to a "Crispy Flounder" at Market Street's Garibaldi's. Fish was not exactly my thing after three years of not much else, but I acquiesced. Was I glad I did. After being deep-fried, a whole flounder is then coated in an apricot-cilantro glaze. I realized right then that fish and sweet sauces are a marriage at the altar of the palate. This chutney is not heavy like the coatings described above, but rather it offers the lightness of tropical fruit along with the natural sweetness of honey plus many of the traditional flavors used when preparing seafood.

CANNING NOTES
- **This is an acidified hot-pack recipe.**
- **pH is low; a safety check before canning will suffice.**
- **This recipe makes 8 half-pint jars; jar size does not matter.**
- **This recipe cannot be halved easily but can be doubled or multiplied.**

INGREDIENTS
1 pineapple, skinned and small-diced
2 mangos, skinned, seeded, and small-diced
4 kiwis, skinned, sliced, and slices halved
1 medium red onion, medium-diced
1 cup water
1½ cups honey
1½ cups sugar
½ cup freshly squeezed lime juice
¼ cup grated fresh ginger
2 tablespoons minced garlic
1 tablespoon coarsely ground pepper
1 tablespoon crushed red pepper; or 1 to 3 hot peppers of choice, finely diced
½ tablespoon celery seed

DIRECTIONS
Place the prepared fruits and onion in a non-reactive pot with the water and bring to a boil. Reduce heat and cook until water is nearly gone.

Add the remaining ingredients and, stirring often to prevent burning, cook on medium high until the chutney shows signs of thickening. Bring to 190 degrees F.

Hot-pack and seal in sterile jars. Invert for 2 minutes minimum.

SERVING SUGGESTIONS
Salmon is a favorite for this chutney, although Arctic char and steelhead trout are extravagant substitutes when available. Farm-raised salmon and char can be purchased from responsible fisheries featuring clean, healthy, sea-based farms producing an excellent product. But when the opportunity arises, always choose the wild. There is no equal. A fish that has survived in the wild has real muscle (meat) unlike a fish that has been leisurely swimming in a circle with not a care in the world. I speak of pink-fleshed fish, a condition created by diet, not birth. But white fish like flounder works equally well, and the fish does not have to come from the sea. Mountain and lake trout as well as catfish, pike, pickerel, and walleye will score high marks with

this chutney. Just bypass fishy fish-like cod and mackerel. All you need to do is ladle a table-spoon or two on top of each fish serving after it comes off the heat.

A 1-pound fillet takes about 25 minutes in a 325-degree oven, less under the broiler or on the grill. Smother the chutney over the fish just as it is removed from the broiler and allow it to finish for 5 minutes. The flavors will set and the various colors against the flesh make an attractive presentation. This is a light meal, not a meat-and-potatoes kind of evening, so quinoa (the ancient grain of the Inca; a light, complex starch with a perfect protein complement) might be an excellent choice. Along with the 2:1 water/quinoa mix, add 1 teaspoon of lime juice for each ½ cup of water used. For a vegetable, use one of the dark leafy greens like spinach. Here is a well-balanced dinner with an attractive and colorful presentation in under a half hour.

— pickles —

THE TERM *HOME CANNING* invokes images of cucumber pickles. While these are certainly part of the pickle universe, they are far from the whole. Pickling is simply a method of preserving by using salted brine, vinegars, or both. Salted water extracts water from the cells of produce, substituting salt, while vinegars lower the pH level. In the modern world, we add heat to kill residual bacteria while the ensuing cooling creates a vacuum in a sealed jar.

Not so long ago, barrels filled with seasoned pickling brine and floating cucumbers used to adorn small groceries. It was easy to pluck what you wanted, and off you went—fresh dill pickles ready for the eating. Life was simple back then!

Nearly every community has its favorite pickle recipes. Some are off the wall. Some sound delicious. I'm always on the lookout, and when my eye catches one that might have great value or is unique, I try it and sometimes improve it. If it turns out to be exceptional, I record the results. At other times, life tickles the creative. In a gourmet burger shop not long ago, I was asked if I would like a few jalapeño pepper slices on my cheeseburger. One bite later, I knew a quality pickling brine would improve the pepper, improve the burger, and, as simple as it was, be in this book. So I went to work. Pickles are some of the easiest recipes to produce and each will surpass the quality of commercially available counterparts while reaching heights one desires to achieve. Enjoy this medley.

achar

Achar is the Hindi word for "pickle." It's very popular in the eastern and southern regions of the African continent because of an Indian influence and is possibly the oldest recorded pickle recipe in America dating back to early colonial times. The achar recipe was brought from India by early sea captains running with the trades from the Far East, around the Cape of Good Hope, and on to the little colonies of the New World. Greeted with open arms, there was plenty of need for such a pickle in colonial times. Without refrigeration, the dark cold winter months left tables barren of produce other than a few winter-hardy varieties. This pickle provided some of the nutrients lacking. A bowl of pickled vegetables graced the center of many a colonial dinner table. Smart matrons kept a large stoneware crock in the kitchen filled with pickling brine, and various vegetables were added as they became available. The popularity of achar was instantaneous and has never waned; the recipe has survived more than three hundred years.

CANNING NOTES
- This is an acidified water-bath recipe.
- pH will be below 4.2; if above, something is incorrect. Vinegar with 5 percent acidity is critical; less might create dangerous pH conditions.
- Recipe liquids will make 7 pint jars; pints and quarts are best suited.
- One can make as many jars as desired.

SOAKING SOLUTION
1 cup canning salt
3 quarts cold water

VEGETABLES*
3 carrots, peeled, trimmed to 4-inch lengths, and quartered lengthwise
7 stalks celery, split lengthwise and cut into 3½-inch lengths

21 string beans, stems clipped and trimmed to less than 4 inches
1 head cabbage, heart removed and cut into golf-ball-size chunks
3 small cucumbers, ends trimmed, cut to 4-inch lengths and quartered
1 cauliflower, broken into silver-dollar-size florets
14 radishes
3 small onions, peeled and quartered
21 cloves garlic
4 Brussels sprouts, halved

PICKLING SOLUTION
5 cups cider vinegar
2 teaspoons turmeric
½ cup peeled and cut fresh ginger (½-inch-thick medallions)
2 tablespoons whole yellow mustard seeds
¼ cup red pepper flakes

DIRECTIONS

To soak the vegetables, dissolve salt in the cold water. Place prepared vegetables in the solution and soak for 24 hours in the refrigerator or in a cool location; drain but do not rinse.

Start the next procedure by making sure each jar gets its fair share by placing one of each of the ten vegetables in each jar until all the vegetables are used or the jars are filled to the canning line and packed tight. Nothing should be above the canning line.

Mix together the pickling solution and bring to a strong boil for 5 minutes. Place the jars in the canning rack; fill, starting with the center jar (cold jar). Check pH of liquid in center jar.

Loosely lid the jars except place the special lid with thermometer (see page 23) on the center jar. Carefully lower into the boiling water, ensuring the water level does not come higher than the fill line (see page 15). When boiling begins again, lower heat so water remains just below boiling.

When thermometer records 190 degrees F, wait 2 minutes, remove, replace lid on thermometer jar, tighten all lids, and invert for 2 minutes minimum.

4-inch trimmings are recommended so that long vegetables can stand in a pint jar. If canning quarts, longer pieces can be used.

SERVING SUGGESTIONS

I like to cross-slice one, some, or sometimes all of the various pickled vegetables to add to a salad. The flavors make for a unique addition, plus much color is added.

In days gone by, families would have a bowl of these bright pickles on the table to pass around along with other condiments. This still works today. The acids in achar aid digestion while leaving behind an alkaline ash from the cider vinegar, offsetting many of the acid-ash portions of a meal that hinder good health. A body with a natural pH of 7.0 or above might remain healthier. Lower than this is an engraved invitation to many diseases. When we dig deep using the shovel of modern science, we often uncover intelligent reason, although unexplainable at the time, for the whys of how people once ate. It is not hard to believe that 50,000 generations passing down experience got it right.

summer squash pickle

There are numerous recipes for preserving the delicate flavors of summer. There is not a farmers market goes by when someone doesn't ask for a pickle of this description. It is understandable. These are so tasty that one would think them common, and yet they are difficult to find in local markets and impossible to find on supermarket shelves. The reason? The squash have a narrow summer window, and they are—what do we say—common, plain vanilla, no pizzazz! Often in my writing, I refer to simple as sometimes being the best, including living. This pickle is no exception.

CANNING NOTES
- **This is an acidified water-bath recipe.**
- **At time of the water bath, process pH of liquids must be below 4.3.**
- **This recipe makes 7 pint jars; pints are best suited.**
- **This recipe can be halved, doubled, or multiplied.**

VEGETABLES
7 cups cubed yellow summer squash (1-inch pieces)
3 cups crosscut zucchini (sections no more than 1 inch thick)
1½ cups medium-diced red onion
2½ cups medium-diced red bell pepper
2 carrots, crosscut into 1-inch pieces, then halved or quartered
7 cloves garlic (1 for each jar)

SALTWATER SOLUTION
1 quart water mixed with ¾ cup salt

PICKLING SOLUTION
2½ cups cider vinegar
2 cups sugar
2 teaspoons whole celery seed
1 teaspoon dry mustard

DIRECTIONS

In a pot, glass baking dish, or other large-surfaced container, spread out the squash and onion; sprinkle salt on top and leave for 2 hours minimum.

When ready to proceed, add saltwater solution, stir the vegetables once, and drain well but do not rinse. Mix all the vegetables together except the garlic. Put 1 garlic clove in each sterile jar and then fill with the remaining vegetables.

Prepare the pickling solution by mixing all ingredients together in a nonreactive pot, place over heat, and bring to a boil.

Place the jars in the canning rack, fill with the solution, center jar first (cold jar), and check the pH of the liquid. Place the thermometer in the center jar with the special lid, loosely lid the other jars and lower into the boiling bath, ensuring the water level does not come higher than the fill line (see page 15) on the jars. As the water begins to return to a boil, lower heat slightly to prevent further boiling.

When canning temperature of 200 degrees F is reached, wait 2 minutes before removing jars. Tighten lids, replace center lid, and invert all jars for 2 minutes minimum.

SERVING SUGGESTIONS

Not all canned items go on or beside something else; some stand alone. The dill pickle is a perfect example. In the South, jars of pickled okra are often seen at college football games. Summer squash pickle is neither a stand-alone nor a put-on-top-of, yet it goes just fine being put on top of rice or next to a potato or in a salad. It also finds a very comfortable place on a plate just sitting all by itself, ready to add its thing to whatever the meal designer has prepared. Sometimes it's the sweet that's lacking on the plate; sometimes it's cheerful colors; sometimes when it's cold and the sky is battleship gray, we need a reminder that summer will come.

pickled brussels sprouts

It was in the fall of 2008 that I was in Santa Cruz visiting my best friend. On dirt bikes, we explored the coastal cliffs that hold back the mighty Pacific. A little north we happened upon a farm harvesting Brussels sprouts. I learned only then while looking at the plants that sprouts were not baby cabbages. Many recipes use sugar. I thought I'd give sugar a rest. I'm glad I did. Crisp and invigorating with nothing bad going into the body makes for even better eating.

CANNING NOTES
- **This is an acidified water-bath recipe.**
- **pH of liquid at time of water bath cannot exceed 4.2. If higher (and this should not be), check percentage solution of cider vinegar first; it must be 5 percent. Second, recheck with new pH paper in clear natural sunlight. If above 4.2, pour out pickling solution, make a new batch, and continue to process after taking a pH test.**
- **This recipe's pickling solution makes 7 jars; pints are best suited.**
- **Solution amounts can be halved, doubled, or multiplied.**

SOAKING SOLUTION
1 cup pure or canning salt
2 quarts water

INGREDIENTS
1 clove garlic, ends trimmed
½ tablespoon dill weed
½ teaspoon mustard seed
¼ teaspoon whole celery seed
7 (8-ounce) Brussels sprouts, wilted outer petals removed, ends trimmed, soaked

PICKLING SOLUTION
8 cups cider vinegar
2 cups water
¼ cup salt
1 to 2 tablespoons red pepper flakes

DIRECTIONS
Mix together the salt and water. Place the sprouts in the saltwater solution for 3 hours before removing and rinsing.

Sterilize and load jars with the ingredients, sprouts last, and place in the canning rack.

Mix the pickling solution ingredients together and boil for 3 minutes, allowing the heat of the pepper flakes to permeate the solution. It will begin to redden.

Fill the jars (cold jar first) to the canning lines, loosely attach the lids, put the thermometer with special lid on the cold jar, and lower into water bath, making sure the level of water does not exceed the canning line of the jars. When the water begins to boil for a second time, lower the heat slightly to prevent further boiling.

When jars reach 200 degrees F, wait 2 minutes before removing. Tighten lids, replace and tighten thermometer lid, and invert all for required 2 minutes minimum.

SERVING SUGGESTIONS

Eating pickled Brussels sprouts right out of the jar is not a bad thing. Providing it as a substitute pickle for a tuna sandwich will go a long way in demonstrating one's individuality. Or partially slice one and fit it on the rim in lieu of the obligatory celery stalk when serving a Bloody Mary; maybe call it Bloody Mary visits Brussels. Call it what you may, it will be called "unique." For other uses, just think dill pickle and substitute, or quarter a few sprouts to add to an evening salad; its uses are endless.

bread-and-butter pickles

My first book, *Putting Up,* had a popular recipe that ruled for most of the twentieth century. There's no doubt why the pickle's popularity continues into the twenty-first century. Is it tradition, taste, or usage? The answer is "yes" to all three. Even when I'm serving a simple supper, if nothing else from the pantry finds its way beside or on top of a serving, I'll place a small heap of B&B pickles somewhere on the plate. The acid aids digestion, the sweet puts a smile on every face, and the pickle flavors act as an ambassador, bringing together the starch, protein, and vegetable of a single meal into harmonious accord.

CANNING NOTES
- **This is an acidified water-bath recipe.**
- **pH will be below 4.2 if balsamic vinegar is used.**
- **The solution mix is for 7 pint jars; pints and half pints work best.**
- **The solution can be halved, doubled, or multiplied.**

VEGETABLES
4 pounds pickling cucumber,* ends trimmed, thin-sliced

3 medium white or yellow onions, thin-sliced, slices halved

2 red bell peppers, medium-diced

PREPARATION
¾ cup pure salt

3 pounds ice

PICKLING SOLUTION
3 cups white balsamic vinegar

2 cups honey

3 jalapeños (or pepper of heat choice), minced

3 cloves garlic, minced

1 tablespoon mustard seed

2 teaspoons celery seed

2 teaspoons pickling spices or whole cloves

DIRECTIONS
Spread the cucumbers, onions, and peppers in a large flat pan, sprinkle with the salt and cover with the ice. Wait 3 hours, or until the ice has melted before draining well. Do not rinse. Gently but firmly pack the cucumber mélange into sterile jars.

Prepare the pickling solution and bring to a boil. In the canning rack, fill the jars, loosely lid, insert the thermometer, and heat in the water bath to 190 degrees F following water bath protocol (see page 15).

Wait 2 minutes, remove, tighten lids, replace thermometer lid, and invert for 2 minutes minimum.

SERVING SUGGESTIONS
This is one of those put-up delights that can lead you to the end of your imagination and beyond. There is nothing quite like a genuine homemade bread-and-butter pickle nestled within the bun of a hamburger or cheeseburger just off the backyard grill. And while on the topic of adding to, try taking a few of these sweet acidic discs along with the accompanying onions and bell peppers, rough-chop them, and add to a salad. Even with the touch of heat, which is a choice, kids love 'em. It's amazing what a finicky child will consume with a sweetened pickle on top.

*Pickling cucumbers are smaller and therefore the seeds inside are small, a definite consideration but most important when not picking from one's own garden or buying from a farmers market. Also, pickling cucumbers are not waxed. Waxed won't work!

salsas

SALSA MEANS "SAUCE" in Spanish and was so named by the discovering conquistadors as they plundered Central America where the tomato and the hot pepper had been cultivated for thousands of years. Today, if there are two items that have altered the distribution of shelf space within American grocery markets, they are salsas and accompanying chips; where once a brand or two of each sufficed, today entire aisles are dedicated to the hundreds. As of the year 2000, salsa supplanted ketchup as the number one selling sauce. This phenomenal new addiction partially has to do with the discovery that we have southern neighbors. Over several decades, the wonderful cuisines south of the border have pushed north until we find these foods completely integrated into our diet today.

Not unlike all that has come before in this volume, using fresh produce always makes the best. Reading the ingredients on jars of store-bought distant cousins will spill the beans: dried this and that, and the word "tomato" is followed by a parenthesis with a list inside signifying that the item has been processed along with the other listed ingredients. Home-produced salsas made entirely with fresh ingredients will be the hit of any game-day get-together regardless of the teams or score, so be certain to make enough for the season, running out only AFTER Super Bowl Sunday.

Within these next several pages, you will be afforded the opportunity to produce something unlike any major grocer has ever carried or ever will carry, or any big manufacturer has even attempted to make. There is nearly a war over shelf space when it comes to salsa, yet nothing beats fresh or home-canned. It makes no sense to purchase. Salsas are simple to produce. Fresh is key, so make them when fruits and vegetables are ripe and straight from the ground when tastes are richest. In the hot section, there are a couple of simple hot sauces. For those seeking a hotter salsa, maybe with deliberate intent, make the salsas palatable for a wider range and have a homemade hot sauce to fire up the mix when demanded.

triple-six fruit salsa

The first time I created this, it was not for canning purposes. It was mid-July and mangos were plentiful among the open-air markets. So much positive feedback followed that I whipped up batch after batch, making this a super summer salsa. As fall approached, the fresh, soft, ripe fruit began fading from the markets, and I vowed I would not wait through three seasons for my summer salsa. I began to work on a recipe that would put up well and remain fresh-tasting. With the pop of a vacuum-sealed canning lid, summer salsa at its near finest could be had. Each time I serve this salsa, even if it's snowing out-side, from somewhere distant and carried on a summer breeze across the seasons, I hear Gershwin's "Summertime" playing just around a corner. The livin' is easy!

CANNING NOTES
- This is an acidified hot-pack recipe.
- pH should be below 3.8; if higher, adjust canning temperature accordingly.
- This recipe makes 6 pints; pints are best suited.
- This recipe can be halved, doubled, or multiplied.

INGREDIENTS
6 mangoes, peeled, seeded, and medium-chopped
6 limes, peeled, sliced, seeded, and slices quartered
6 tomatoes, cut in half, seeded, squeezed, and medium-chopped
2 cups medium-diced white onion
1/2 cup finely diced green bell pepper
1/4–1/2 cup deveined, seeded, and minced hot pepper of choice
3 cloves garlic, minced
3/4 cup freshly squeezed lime juice
1/4 cup sugar
2 teaspoons salt
1/2 cup finely chopped fresh cilantro

DIRECTIONS
Temperature is the critical measurement here. Like all canned products with a pH below 3.8, final canning must not take place below 182 degrees F. But every degree above that critical number diminishes the freshness of the flavors, especially the savory cilantro, so make sure your thermometer is calibrated (see page 23).

In a nonreactive pot, place all but the cilantro and bring the mixture to 185 degrees F. Add the cilantro and blend well. Next, ensure the pH is at the 3.8 threshold for canning at 182 degrees F.

Add three degrees for jar cooling (185 degrees F.) before pouring into sterilized jars. Seal and invert for 2 minutes minimum.

SERVING SUGGESTIONS
Twenty years ago, it might have taken a rocket scientist to figure out that chips go with salsa, but no longer. Salsa and chips, however, are only a first baby step in the beginning journey with salsas. Try ladling some over delicate white fish like perch, over roast chicken, over scrambled eggs, or by adding a touch to salads for a fruity addition. If it works, do it—convention has not a thing to do with good tasting.

cherry salsa

Cherry season is a time in summer to remember. One cannot stop eating those delicious fruits. In many parts of our country, it is a time for festival and celebration as the big crops are harvested. In the jams section, I have included a cherry preserve that will heighten a family breakfast, and in the chutney section is a recipe for maybe a spectacular dinner. But cherries are definitely a grand enough fruit to deserve an all-around everyday recipe, and what better way to serve and honor them than with a salsa?

CANNING NOTES

- This is an acidified hot-pack recipe.
- pH will be below 4.2 if all and accurately measured ingredients are used.
- This recipe makes 6 or 7 half-pint jars; pint and half pints best serve this recipe.
- This recipe can be doubled or multiplied.

INGREDIENTS

4 cups pitted and halved sweet cherries
2 cups seeded and squeezed, medium-chopped vine-ripened tomatoes
1 cup medium-diced white onion
¼ cup seeded, deveined, and finely chopped jalapeño (or pepper of choice)
¼ cup freshly squeezed lemon juice
3 tablespoons honey
1 tablespoon balsamic vinegar
2 cloves garlic, minced
1 teaspoon pepper
1 teaspoon salt
1 cup finely chopped, tightly packed fresh cilantro

DIRECTIONS

Place all of the ingredients except the cilantro in a nonreactive canning pot. Stirring often, bring to 190 degrees F; add cilantro and check pH before ladling into sterile jars.

Lid, seal, and invert for 2 minutes minimum.

SERVING SUGGESTIONS

As a salsa with chips, this is a hero: unique, using all fresh produce, and blending so many flavors. All will enjoy. Store-bought salsas will become not only a memory but a bad dream.

Aside from the usual suspects that work and are limited only by imagination, chicken salad with cherry salsa over the top makes an out-of-this-world luncheon serving.

corn and black-eyed pea salsa

Sometimes referred to as Texas Caviar but always touted as delicious, this salsa is just as comfortable next to a plate of chips as it is on a dinner plate. The traditional salsa tastes of tomato, onion, and peppers are enhanced with the sweetness of fresh corn and given extra body by the peas, making this a special treat that can be used for many different occasions.

CANNING NOTES
- This is an acidified hot-pack recipe.
- pH needs to be kept below 4.3. Each batch of beans acidifies differently. Monitor closely. To lower, add additional vinegar or, if too liquid, add citric acid $\frac{1}{4}$ teaspoon at a time.
- The recipe will make 6 or 7 pint jars; pints and half pints are best suited.
- The recipe can be halved, doubled, or multiplied.

INGREDIENTS
4 cups dried black-eyed peas
4 cups corn (cut off the cob)
3 cups cider vinegar, divided

3 cups seeded and squeezed, medium-chopped tomatoes
1 cup finely diced red onion
$\frac{1}{2}$ cup medium-diced red bell pepper
$\frac{1}{2}$ cup medium-diced green bell pepper
3 cloves garlic, minced
$\frac{1}{4}$ cup red pepper flakes
2 cups sugar
1 cup freshly squeezed lime juice
2 tablespoons olive oil
1 teaspoon ground cumin
1 teaspoon coarsely ground pepper
1 teaspoon salt
$\frac{1}{4}$ cup finely chopped cilantro

DIRECTIONS
Put the dried peas in a pot, cover with 4 inches of water, and bring to a boil. Turn off heat and allow to stand overnight. Drain, rinse, add fresh water; return to a boil, lower, and heat until peas are softening; drain and rinse well before measuring 4 cups.

Place the peas and corn in a bowl with 1 cup cider vinegar, mix well, and allow to acidify for 1 hour before draining.

Put remaining vinegar and ingredients except the cilantro in a nonreactive pot and bring to a canning temperature of 200 degrees F. Add the cilantro, stir to distribute well before checking pH, and adjust if necessary.

Fill sterile jars, seal, and invert for 2 minutes minimum.

SERVING SUGGESTIONS
Thus far, this volume seldom mentions red meat. It is not that this writer has an aversion, but the true flavor of steak can be destroyed if not treated only with toppings or sides that truly complement it. If there ever was a salsa that complemented steak, this might be it. It is interesting that such a meat-friendly salsa is referred to as Texas Caviar, not a state known for its herds of chicken; with her longhorn cattle, Texas was the beef center of the Old West.

To complement a steak dinner, try brown rice,

a complex carbohydrate. Unlike a baked potato or white rice, the stored energy is released over a prolonged period, making it a healthier choice.

Another little-known substitute for the baked potato is baked Jerusalem artichokes. This starch is a complex carbohydrate as well as a source of excellent probiotic enrichment. Instead of butter, try ladling this salsa over the top of either one. It also complements cooked greens equally well. The rest is left to innate potential. Go for it!

balsamic vinegar tomato salsa

One afternoon in Santa Cruz, while visiting my best friend and his wife, Colleen, I was introduced to this modified beaten-path recipe. I don't know why, but inside that western edge of America, many think outside the box. It is refreshing! Colleen had made a simple salsa but used balsamic vinegar instead. The incredible flavors haunted as I winged my way east, so much so that I knew it would have to be in this book.

It's close to a traditional tomato salsa recipe, but where the traditional fresh or canned gets a splash of acid with lemon or lime juice and/or cider vinegar, this salsa gets the flavorful Italian crown jewel. One does not have to spend a fortune on the vinegar used. Prices for quality balsamic can be far higher than prized wines; but for cooking, the lesser priced works just fine.

CANNING NOTES

- **This is an acidified hot-pack recipe.**
- **pH will be below 4.2; to reduce, add additional vinegar 2 tablespoons at a time.**
- **The recipe makes 6 pint jars; pints and half pints best serve this recipe.**
- **The recipe can be halved, doubled, or multiplied.**

INGREDIENTS

9 cups seeded, squeezed, and chopped tomatoes
3 cups finely diced white onion
1 cup medium-diced green bell pepper
1 (12-ounce) can tomato paste (see page 34 for special prep treatment)
½ cup balsamic vinegar
¼ cup honey
¼ cup minced garlic
¼ cup seeded and minced jalapeño (or pepper of choice)
2 tablespoons olive oil
2 teaspoons salt
½ tablespoon pepper
½ cup finely chopped fresh cilantro

DIRECTIONS

Place all of the ingredients except cilantro in a nonreactive canning pot and bring to 190 degrees F. Add cilantro, stir in, and check pH.

Pour into sterile jars, seal, and invert for 2 minutes minimum.

SERVING SUGGESTIONS

Because of the black vinegar, I like to use the whiter variety of chips to further the mystic of a unique salsa. Try making scrambled eggs with cheddar or multiple cheeses mixed in and serve with this salsa poured over the top. Finishing a baked, broiled, or grilled piece of light fish always works for salsa, so why not try a tuna salad with the balsamic salsa blended into the salad and served on a bed of greens or stuffed into a pita pocket? There is a start, take it from there.

soups

THE LACK OF ACID in vegetables limits the canning of many soups without using pressure, but it doesn't mean the ones we can make won't be exceptional. These soups are special, unique, and safe. When producing soups, we are often canning above pH 4.0, so it is imperative to prepare with care, to test and retest. These recipes are safe if the ingredients are proper and the measurements accurate.

When you're exhausted yet hungry, it is always a pleasant feeling to know that within a few moments you can be having a steaming bowl of delicious, healthy, and flavorful homemade soup. As an added bonus, the maker will know it will not be over-salted, and there are none of those unheard of chemicals none of us can even pronounce mixed among freeze-dried onions and this and that. And on hot summer evenings when the thought of a big dinner is beyond comprehension, there is little more refreshing than a light supper consisting of a bowl of chilled soup, a salad, and a break of bread.

Soups are mostly canned in quarts because they typically serve four, but pints work wonderfully for those quiet evenings at home alone, so consider making both when it comes to soup, and make several runs. When friends get sick, a jar of soup makes for an easy trouble-free meal. A quart of homemade soup also makes a perfect house gift and is far more considerate and caring than a bottle of wine. In the last chapter of this book, there will be suggestions on how to customize such a splendid gift.

black bean soup

Black bean soup is something to adore. After a hard day of work when I need just enough to cut the edge off the day's hunger, I heat up a can of my favorite soup and enjoy it with a freshly baked small loaf and an excellent quality butter. One by one, those great cans of yesterday have vanished from market shelves. Today we are left with gourmet, they say, but it tastes marginal at best. In the past, I never could bring myself to create something better than what was so good, but now a void demands filling. Here we go!

CANNING NOTES
- This is an acidified hot-pack recipe.
- pH is critical; maintaining pH below 4.3 is detailed in recipe instructions.
- This recipe makes 4 quarts; pints and quarts work best.
- This recipe can be halved, doubled, or multiplied.

INGREDIENTS
4 pounds dry black beans (12 cups prepared beans)
2 cups finely chopped onion
2 cups finely chopped celery
2 cups finely chopped carrots
2 cups chicken or vegetable broth
¾ cup finely chopped red bell pepper
¾ cup finely chopped green bell pepper
1 cup olive oil
1 cup cider vinegar
½ cup lemon juice
¼ cup sherry (optional)
2 tablespoons salt
12 cloves garlic, minced
12 bay leaves, boiled in 2 cups water*
½ cup orange juice
½ cup sugar
2 teaspoons dry mustard
1 teaspoon cayenne powder
1 teaspoon citric acid

DIRECTIONS
Prepare the dried black beans the day before: rinse the beans, place them in a pot with water covering twice the depth of the beans, bring to a boil, turn off, and allow to sit overnight.

Rinse, put in new water, and bring to a boil. Cook until soft and then rinse well. Measure 12 cups, discarding the balance. Add the beans to a nonreactive canning pot along with all other ingredients except the citric acid. Heat the soup to 160 degrees F before making the first of TWO pH tests. If pH is above 4.2, lower by adding 2 tablespoons vinegar plus 2 teaspoons orange juice and 1 teaspoon lemon juice. If still too high, add ¼ teaspoon citric acid at a time and continue until pH is at 4.2.

In a blender or food processor, purée the soup several cups at a time. When complete, return to pot and bring to canning temperature of 210 degrees F. Check pH a second time. (This is a most important check since all the ingredients have been opened by the purée process.) To reduce to 4.2, first add ¼ teaspoon citric acid. Stir in well and check pH. If necessary, do one more time. If pH still requires lowering, add 2 tablespoons cider vinegar, 1 tablespoon orange juice, and 2 teaspoons sugar until pH is correct.

Maintain the canning temperature of 210 degrees, pour in sterile jars, seal, and invert for 2 minutes minimum.

SERVING SUGGESTIONS

Black bean soup can be either a spectacular first course or a complete dinner. For a first course, it is a rich soup and, based upon dinner, you will have to decide how much to serve— either a ramekin or a small soup bowl. A dollop of sour cream in the center is attractive and adds to the flavor; and a slice of lemon attached to the side of the bowl comes off well, the acid working its magic.

For a supper, along with the sour cream and the lemon slice, pour in a ½ ounce of quality sherry and sprinkle cheddar cheese on top. Serve it with a roll or a baguette. There is little else needed to be content.

Boil the bay leaves in the water for 10 minutes; add additional water if necessary. When complete, discard the leaves and then add the water to the recipe.

burnt sweet potato soup

I owe the descriptive "burnt" to a farmers market patron. Thank you! She suggested it because I had overcooked the potatoes, and the caramelized sugars that oozed out made the flavors of this soup even better. Now, we always overcook the potatoes when preparing them. Rich in vitamins A and C, with excellent portions of fiber, protein, potassium, and beta carotene, this complex carbohydrate—the simple sweet potato—alone can sustain life for many, many months on end. The Center for Science in Public Interest (CSPI) ranks the sweet potato nutritionally as the highest eatable vegetable Americans consume by over one hundred points. With credentials like this, it is only fitting that we make a few jars of this soup to serve on frosty fall and winter days. It doesn't get much healthier nor taste better beginning with autumn's cool.

CANNING NOTES
- **This is an acidified hot-pack recipe.**
- **pH must be below 4.3, which is critical. To reduce, add 1 tablespoon lime juice and 1 tablespoon cider vinegar at a time until pH is 4.2.**
- **This recipe makes 5+ quart jars; pints and quarts work best.**
- **This recipe can be halved, but doubling can become overwhelming.**

INGREDIENTS
12 cups mashed baked sweet potatoes* (about 9 pounds)
4 cups Granny Smith apples
2 cups freshly squeezed orange juice (pulp included)
¼ cup freshly squeezed lime juice
2 cups fresh apple juice
3 tablespoons finely diced fresh ginger
¼ cup dark brown sugar
½ cup honey
3 tablespoons butter
1½ tablespoons cinnamon
2 teaspoons allspice
1 tablespoon vanilla extract
1 tablespoon salt
15+ cups water or ham stock (enough to thin recipe to soup consistency)**

DIRECTIONS
Bake the sweet potatoes (about ¾ to 1 pound each) in a 425 degree F oven until the centers are soft when skewered with a fork and the skins show the first signs of burning, about 1 hour and 20 minutes.

Peel and core the apples and bake with the sweet potatoes just until soft, about 20 minutes. After the sweet potatoes are done, mash or purée them with the apples, fruit juices, and ginger.

Put all ingredients except the water or stock in a nonreactive canning pot. Over medium heat, slowly add the remaining liquid, mixing well while keeping below boiling. Continue adding water or stock, reducing thickness until soup reaches the desired consistency (or make a concentrated product to be thinned before serving).

Cook for 10 minutes. Perform a preliminary pH test. This is critical and pH may require adjusting (see canning note above for guidance). Bring pot to canning temperature of 205 degrees F. Be extra cautious. The soup will bubble and splatter as it approaches a boil. Unlike a splattered drop of water, this thick, hot soup is more akin to

molten lava and can cause severe burns.

Finally, hot-pack in sterile jars, seal with sterile lids, and invert completed jars for 2 minutes minimum.

SERVING SUGGESTIONS

Being so nutritious, this soup can stand alone as a simple yet hearty and healthy meal. Accompanied with a salad, few simple and quick meals can compare.

When preparing the soup as a complete meal, consider adding a little cream, float a pat of butter in the center of the bowl, and make a squiggly design with dark brown sugar. Kids and adults alike will lick their bowls.

In a more formal setting, offer it as the soup course. It is rich and, since we expect our guests to eat their dinners, serve in a ramekin instead of a bowl, with a lime on the edge while holding off on the butter, cream, and brown sugar design.

There are two common varieties of sweet potatoes grown in the United States and found at farmers markets, at roadside markets, and in groceries. The one you don't want to use has a light skin and yellowish meat, which becomes dry and crumbly like that of a regular baking potato when cooked. Look for the darker garnet-skinned variety with a deep orange meat, which is moist and mushy when cooked.

**Water may be used in this recipe instead of ham stock since meat, especially ham, offends some. Plus there is no low sodium ham base readily available. So either use store bought and eliminate the salt in the recipe or make your own. In either case, when using stock, it must be reduced to pH 4.2 by adding cider vinegar, a tablespoon at a time prior to being added to the recipe.*

butternut squash soup

Fall not only begins the season of soup, it is also the season of squash—pumpkin, acorn, and butternut, to name a few. Once you have mastered the canning principle of pH control, then you are ready to put up this delicious yet complex repast. Canned thick, it can be reduced with cream, milk, or water to the serving consistency most appealing to the user. There is a theory, and it makes sense, that if one eats produce within the season of harvest, the body is in natural harmony with its caloric and nutritional needs for the coming months. Butternut is a fall/winter squash, making this recipe ideal as a chilly evening supper.

CANNING NOTES

- This is an acidified hot-pack recipe.
- Initial pH must be below 4.3; lower pH by adding lime juice 2 tablespoons at a time. If necessary, add ¼ teaspoon citric acid.
- This recipe makes 4 quart jars; Jar size does not matter.
- This recipe can be doubled or multiplied.

INGREDIENTS

9 cups butternut squash (3 or 4 medium squash)

6 cups low-sodium chicken broth (vegetable or vegan broths work too)

¾ cup butter, melted

6 tablespoons flour

3 cups finely chopped red onion

6 Granny Smith apples, peeled, cored, baked, and puréed

¼ cup honey

½ cup cider vinegar

1½ cups orange juice

1½ cups lemon juice

1½ teaspoons pepper

1½ teaspoons salt

2 teaspoons cinnamon

1 teaspoon mace

1 teaspoon coriander

3 tablespoons grated fresh ginger

DIRECTIONS

Split the butternut squash lengthwise, scoop out the seeds, and bake in a 400-degree oven for 30 to 40 minutes, until the meat is soft throughout. Scoop out the insides and discard the skins. Mash well or purée with some of the broth to ensure the squash is not lumpy. If you do not have a food processor, a potato masher will work fine. For safety reasons, the soup MUST be lump-free.

Make a paste with the butter and flour. Place remaining ingredients in a nonreactive pot, bring to 210 degrees F (not quite boiling), and take the initial pH test (VERY important); adjust until pH is 4.2.

When pH is correct, pour into sterile jars, seal, and invert for 2 minutes minimum.

SERVING SUGGESTIONS

The flavor of the soup is exceptional yet sophisticated. The yellowish green orange can be best accented by floating a few tarragon or thyme leaves in the center of each bowl; either herb is a natural with butternut.

A small cup of soup makes an elegant first course at an in-home dinner party. Seldom more than a 4-ounce serving is necessary, which translates to 8 servings to a quart. If four is a comfortable entertaining number, then put up a few pint jars.

For a dinner soup, serve with a freshly baked multigrain boule topped with a quality butter. There is little that is simpler or better. With suppers like this, many might wish for winter year-round.

tomato-basil soup

There are many recipes for this delicious soup, but only a handful can be found in canning guides. I enjoy working with tomatoes because their natural acidity allows one to become creative without having a major acidification program added to the product. This becomes really important with soups. Nobody wants to sit down to battery acid. The other wonderful thing about tomato soups is that they are generally good either hot or cold. This one is no exception. With many subtle flavors supporting the predominant tomato and basil, this soup becomes a first-class addition to a pantry and will be used year-round.

CANNING NOTES
- This is an acidified hot-pack recipe.
- Initial pH will be below 4.3; to reduce pH, add $\frac{1}{2}$ tablespoon lemon juice and 1 tablespoon balsamic vinegar; stir well and measure again. Continue until pH is 4.2.
- This recipe makes 4+ quarts; pints and quarts best serve this recipe.
- This recipe can be halved, doubled, or multiplied.

INGREDIENTS
2$\frac{1}{2}$ cups finely chopped white onion
2 cloves garlic, minced
4 teaspoons finely minced fresh ginger
$\frac{1}{4}$ cup butter
$\frac{1}{4}$ cup olive oil
6 pounds freshly picked ripe tomatoes, peeled, cored, seeded, and puréed
2 tablespoons freshly squeezed lemon juice
$\frac{1}{4}$ cup balsamic vinegar
2 teaspoons honey
3 cups low-sodium chicken or vegetarian broth
3 cups tomato juice
4 teaspoons salt
2 tablespoons coarsely ground pepper
1 cup finely chopped, tightly packed basil

DIRECTIONS
Sauté the onion, garlic, and ginger in a pan with the butter and olive oil until the onion is clear, about 6 minutes. Purée and put in a nonreactive pot with remaining ingredients except the basil; simmer for 15 minutes, stirring often to prevent burning. Bring the soup to a canning temperature of 205 degrees F. Add the basil, blending in well before checking to ensure pH is below 4.3.

Reduce heat and promptly fill prepared sterile jars. Seal and invert jars for 2 minutes minimum.

SERVING SUGGESTIONS
This is a year-around soup. In the summer, serve it chilled. In the winter, heat it and add 2 tablespoons heavy cream for each 8-ounce serving.

Or to get really fancy, serve as a bisque by making a roux of 2 tablespoons flour whisked into $\frac{1}{4}$ cup melted butter; add to the quart of soup while heating. In all cases, place a leaf or two (or, even better, a star design) of fresh basil in the center of each bowl. Accompany with a simple baguette, and enjoy a completely satisfying and nutritious meal.

As a first course served either hot or cold, use a filled ramekin instead of a half-empty soup bowl. The deep red soup with centered basil leaves forming a star will set the tone for great dining within your gallery of food art.

bouillabaisse

This is by far the most complicated recipe in this book, but it represents the quintessential French fish stew. World-renowned and rightly so, bouillabaisse is seldom seen in its perfected state except in France's coastal communities, simply because it is so time-consuming to produce. Just the same, when canning, one can turn out 6, 12, or even 18 separate dinners in jars in the same time that it would require to fix one bouillabaisse supper from scratch. I took no shortcuts and, although I was forced to strengthen some acid ingredients and cut back on a few of the bases for safe canning, I managed (with the help of a canning angel) to come out with a winner, so much so that I expect to see quart jars selling on the docks of Marseilles along with the catch du jour.

CANNING NOTES

- **This is an acidified hot-pack recipe.**
- **pH is critical and needs to be monitored throughout production; with each pH check, lower to 4.2 with additional white wine.**
- **This recipe makes 6 to 8 quarts; quarts and pints work best.**
- **This recipe can be doubled or multiplied but not halved.**

BROTH INGREDIENTS

16 cloves garlic, medium-chopped
3 cups chopped onion
1 cup chopped celery
20 cups water
4 cups white wine
1 cup olive oil
2 pinches saffron threads steeped in ¼ cup boiling water
10 sprigs thyme
16 whole peppercorns
1 teaspoon salt
1 teaspoon pepper
4+ pounds fish heads, fish tails, shrimp heads. and/or fish carcasses*

BOUILLABAISSE INGREDIENTS

Strained broth from the foregoing ingredients
2 cups chopped leeks, white and lightest of the green sections only
6 pounds blood-red tomatoes, field ripened, seeded, squeezed, and chopped
4 oranges, juice only (reserve rind)
Zest from 2 reserved orange rinds
2 cups chopped, tightly packed fresh fennel, stems and stalks removed
¼ cup minced garlic
1 cup tomato paste
1 cup chopped parsley
½ cup olive oil
2 pinches saffron threads, steeped in ¼ cup dry white wine for 30 minutes in a container floating in near-boiling water
1 onion, finely chopped
6 stalks celery, sliced and diced
4 cups white wine (plus additional wine if necessary to lower pH to 4.2)

DIRECTIONS

Prepare the broth ingredients: place in a nonre-active pot, bring to a boil for 10 minutes, lower heat, check and adjust pH to 4.2, and then simmer for 2 hours, covered. Strain and discard all but the liquid.

Prepare the bouillabaisse ingredients: place in a canning pot with the broth and bring to a boil. Reduce heat and simmer for 30 to 40 minutes, covered. Return to canning temperature of 205 degree F, test pH for second time. If pH needs to be lowered to be safe (4.2 or lower), do so by adding additional white wine.

Mix well to include all ingredients while ladling into sterile jars. Seal and invert for 2 minutes minimum.

SERVING SUGGESTIONS

A French chef will tell you no good bouillabaisse has less than seven different species of fish, not counting shrimp and shellfish. Not so. Six total, including shrimp and all shellfish, is almost over the top, so maybe three or four fish will be more than adequate. Your local fishmonger will help you decide which species will suit best. When it comes to fish, some are hard (as in firm) and some soft, some oily and some not; include some of each. Here are few that work well: salmon, mackerel, grouper, flounder, tilapia, sea bass, scallops, monkfish, lobster (raw), halibut, mahi-mahi (dolphin fish/dorado), eel, whiting, bass. All eatable fish work; however, when making your selections, use no more than two oily types. Then there are the shellfish like little necks, cherry stones, mussels, and, lastly, the shrimp (cooked and peeled). Mussels and shrimp are standards so, just to be totally French, choose one more shellfish if desired for the preparation.

When preparing bouillabaisse for a supper, do a little planning ahead. Cut the fish into 1½ x 1½-inch squares (2 per person), or 2 x 2-inch squares (1 per person); prepare the shrimp (cook and peel, 2 per person); marinate and refrigerate all but the shellfish in olive oil for at least 3 hours; if serving four, use ½ cup with 2 tablespoons minced garlic.

Break the seal on the jar, pour the bouillabaisse into a 6-quart pan, and heat to boiling. Add the oily fish as a rolling boil commences. Immediately reduce heat to medium. After 4 minutes, add the non-oily fish and the shellfish; 3 minutes later add the cooked shrimp. Just 3 minutes more and the stew is ready. Although there is some prior work here, the dinner preparation will take only about a half hour. A quart jar will nicely serve four to six. And remember, no great bouillabaisse is served without a baguette along with the accompanying rouille sauce. This is a meal fit for a Sun God seated at the head of the table at Versailles.

Fish carcasses (the leftovers after filleting) are often available at seafood stores.

brigue onion soup

I might have called this version of the famous and ubiquitous French soup "Border Onion," but the romance of a tiny village that was once in Italy but found itself in France after World War II makes a perfect simile for an onion soup made in the light traditional French style but with the addition of tomato and more onion. Being driven not only by flavor but by final pH, I was finally forced to use a small amount of tomato paste. This changed everything. It drove the pH down to safe levels, brought the color from muddy brown to a pleasing Indian red, and added a sweetness to counter the acidic solution. To further straddle the border, it might be served piping hot with mozzarella on top along with a toasted slice of French baguette sprinkled with grated Parmesan. Oh, so French! Oh, so Italian! Oh, so wonderful! The soup is definitely onion but withholds a harsh onion taste and is denser than the traditional. Smaller portions go further; and one can, if they must, thin it before serving with a little additional beef bouillon. I wouldn't and I don't. Quick to produce and a delight to eat, this recipe will visit my table at least twice monthly.

CANNING NOTES

- **This is an acidified hot-pack recipe.**
- **pH must be lower than 4.3; to reduce pH, add ¼ cup white wine and 2 tablespoons tomato paste at a time.**
- **Recipe makes 4+ quarts; half pints, pints, and quarts all work well.**
- **The recipe may be multiplied or divided.**

INGREDIENTS

1 cup extra virgin olive oil
½ cup butter
9 pounds sweet onions, thinly sliced and then quartered
4 cups beef stock or beef base
2 cups red wine
2 cups white wine
12 ounces tomato paste
2 teaspoons coarsely ground black pepper
4 teaspoons salt

DIRECTIONS

Place the olive oil and butter in a large heavy-bottom pot, big enough to hold the onions with ease so they can be stirred and cooked down. On high, when oil is hot and the butter is melted, add the onions; stirring often, continue to sauté until the onions cook down and begin to brown.

Add the remaining ingredients and, stirring often with burner still on high, heat to boiling. Continue until mixture just begins to thicken. Check pH, 4.2 being highest permissible (to reduce, see canning note above).

Stirring continuously, ladle into sterile jars, seal, and invert for 2 minutes minimum.

SERVING SUGGESTIONS

As a complete yet light repast, heat the soup to very hot and ladle into warmed soup bowls, place thin sliced medallions of fresh mozzarella on the top, and circumscribe the bowl with toasted slices of a baguette accented with Parmesan cheese. It makes a complete meal that is filling, healthy, and full of flavor. But just because the word "soup" is in the title shouldn't cause one's creativity to become limited. Heated and ladled over the evening's protein (like skinless chicken breast, pork chop, or even red meat) is an equally grand usage; maybe sprinkle a little cheese on top. It is why I not only can this in quarts and pints as a soup, but in half pints as a dinner sauce as well.

—all things hot—

THE INFLUENCE OF SPICY FOODS and hot peppers continues to alter our once-bland diets. From the Orient, spiced cooking has been the way for many millennia. And for nearly 400 years and before, such was the case with our neighbors to the south. But until the last quarter of the twentieth century, we Americans (except for Cajun and southwestern border-town dwellers) knew little of the fiery peppers used in cooking. As the lower Americas' hot influence creeps northward, our curiosity heightens and our palates adjust—hot is coming of age. The palate is not alone. Medical research daily finds new cures with capsaicin, the chemical compound in hot peppers that give them the heat.

Witnessing the brisk sales of my spicier products at local farmers markets, I made a 24-jar batch of hot sauce using the recipe from my first book, *Putting Up*. It might well be the hottest sauce anyone has ever tasted, so I figured the two cases would last several months. Wrong! Gone in a morning! The appetite for things hot–hotter–hottest continues to expand. The following day, I decided that instead of having a hot relish in the relish chapter and a hot pickle in the pickle chapter and so forth, I'd combine all things defined by really heavy heat into a single chapter.

Most hot sauces bought are a simple combination of peppers and vinegar. Some manufacturers go so far as to add salt. When complete, the jar cost (not even a quarter) far exceeds the value of the content and labor. The sauce recipes that follow add the missing explosions of flavor, bringing sauces to levels far beyond the pepper and vinegar measuring bar. Some are sweet, some fruity, while others have hints of exotic flavors. There can be a specific hot sauce for every application, even ice cream! Yes, a customer recently confided that she used the hot sauce from my first book over vanilla ice cream. She explained that the fiery hot against the sweet and cold worked wonders on the palate and exposed all the individual mango and orange flavors in the mix. Enjoy them all, but most of all, be proud knowing that you are producing and using a very special product the likes of which are not commercially available.

pickled jalapeños

For those who are into a little heat, this is the pickle. The medallions are the perfect complement for a classic rice and bean dinner. The pepper most used, the jalapeño, measures between 2,500 and 8,000 on the Scoville Scale, appealing to a wide audience of milder heat lovers. Jalapeños are selected over other hotter peppers because of their shape—they are easier to work with, but in the final analysis, it's an individual call. On page 30 is a list of commonly available hot peppers along with their heat rating. If one wants hotter, then go for it, and if the jalapeño singes the palate, there are peppers of lesser heat, one for every palate. The exchange will affect only the heat, not the pH of the finished product.

   When pickling the likes of scotch bonnets, habaneros, or other bulbous peppers, consider cutting the pepper in half from top to bottom and then slice into half rings (not a necessity, just a suggestion). And when pickling whole peppers, it's imperative to make incisions on either side of each pepper. This allows the pickling solution to fully acidify the inside and the outside of the pickled pepper. Safety first, always!

CANNING NOTES

- This is an acidified water-bath recipe.
- Initial pH will be below 4; if above, reduce pH by replacing pickling solution and reducing amount of water by half.
- The solution makes 6 pint jars; both pints and half pints work.
- The solution can be increased for number of jars desired.

JAR INGREDIENTS, PER PINT

1 tablespoon finely chopped yellow onion
1 clove garlic, whole
1 bay leaf
1 tablespoon extra virgin olive oil
2 cups tightly packed sliced jalapeños, 1/4–1/2 inch thick*

PICKLING SOLUTION

6 cups cider vinegar
1 1/2 cups water
3 tablespoons salt
1 to 2 tablespoons sugar (optional—mellows flavor and reduces heat)

DIRECTIONS

Prepare each jar as described.

Bring pickling solution to a boil. Fill jars only to canning line with liquid, loosely apply lids and thermometer lid, immediately lower into water bath ensuring water level does not exceed canning line of jars.

When center jar (cold jar) reaches 185 degrees F, wait 2 minutes, remove rack, replace thermometer lid, tighten all lids, and invert for 2 minutes minimum.

SERVING SUGGESTIONS

When my son and I were wandering the Pacific, we prayed the two lines trailing behind our slow moving sailboat would attract what would become our supper. But this did not always happen. Then it was beans and rice. We dreaded those meals until we discovered pickled jalapeños in a Puerto Escondido *tienda*. The little dime-size medallions altered the bland supper. From that day forward, we "relished" fishless days.

Once or twice a month, I still make our beans and rice dinner. It's good, healthy, and provides me with a pleasant sail down memory lane. Ladle black beans over cooked brown rice (brown provides a more complex carbohydrate), sprinkle some shredded cheddar cheese, add a nice salsa, preferably one you have canned, and then drop a dollop of sour cream on top before sprinkling with pickled jalapeños. Want to go all out? Bake chicken (thighs or breasts) sprinkled with cumin, chili powder, salt, and pepper. Cut into small chunks and spread on the rice with the beans. No matter how this is served—on a plate, on top of a flour tortilla, rolled as a burrito—it makes a fun, delicious yet simple meal. Simple can be elegant. Simple living can be living at its best.

Pickled jalapeños on top of a burger or on a hot dog in a bun jazzes up backyard grilling. These little pickles go as far as one's imagination. Once a jar is opened and refrigerated, the peppers will keep forever, but if you're hot for hot, they won't stay around for long. Instead of an added condiment for burgers, finely chop the peppers and mix into the meat before forming the patties; it will take the "same old" from "same old burgers," while chopped jalapeños added on top of wieners will put a bark into the most boring dog. Add a few chopped pieces into soft cheese for dips and into morning scrambled eggs, or when making a sandwich spread like pimento cheese. Get the picture? The uses for the simplest little pickle just keep on coming.

See note on page 31 about wearing gloves when working with hot peppers.

sizzling strawberry-habanero jam

Taste buds are changing all across America. I can sense it in the pulse of questions at farmers markets where I sell my products. Not long ago and for the first time ever, I was asked if I made a strawberry-habanero jam. "You should." I began to ponder this shift to hot, of which I now write again. My response was still "no"; however, I added, "but I will."

Unlike pickles, where an acid environment keeps the produce from developing toxins, the strawberries in this jam provide sufficient acidity, plus the sugars produce a sugar-saturated environment that pulls the liquid from the peppers to further ensure safety. The fiery heat and the super sweet make a delightful combination, and although I might not have the palate to be ladling gobs of this preserve on a morning biscuit, uses continue to come to me. I call this creation Straw-Banero Jam for short!

CANNING NOTES
- **This is an acidified, sugar-saturated, hot-pack recipe.**
- **pH testing is not required.**
- **This recipe makes 8 half-pint jars; half-pint jars are best suited for this recipe.**
- **This recipe can be doubled but not halved.**

INGREDIENTS
5 cups chopped strawberries
¼ cup lemon juice
1 tablespoon cider vinegar
¼ cup finely chopped habaneros (seeded and deveined first, if desired)
1 pack pectin
½ tablespoon butter (optional—used as an antifoaming agent)
7 cups sugar

DIRECTIONS
Place all but the sugar in a nonreactive pot and bring to a strong rolling boil. Add the sugar, return to a rolling boil (if making a double run, add half the sugar, return to the beginning of a boil, and put in the balance), time for 2 minutes while watching for jelling after 1 minute. When ready, ladle into jars, seal, and invert for 2 minutes only.

SERVING SUGGESTIONS
More people than imagined use this "Hotter than Hades" fruit spread over vanilla ice cream. For me, I'll keep my ice cream cool; but as a spread over a chicken breast, not only does it brighten up the colorless meat, it livens up the eating, turning plain chicken into a heated debate. Often people dribble a bit of hot sauce on eggs, so why not use it when making an omelet with a chunk of Brie cheese? Once the two eggs have begun to firm, plunk the cheese in the middle and ladle 2 tablespoons of the red hot jam over it. Don't forget my discussions interspersed within this book about sweet and meat. Experiment by using this jam with pork, white fish, and even duck. I've tried them all. This heat-adverse writer must tell you that the jam is without fault except straight out of the jar.

apricot-jalapeño jam

An aftertaste of heat (or burn, as some say) is all that is required to add a sense of excitement to a common home-canned recipe and often multiplies the available applications. Apricot jam is no exception. The addition of hot peppers takes this fruit staple beyond the breakfast table and on to all sorts of additional uses from hors d'oeuvres to cooking. By using jalapeños, it is mild hot but still too hot for the jam section; after experimenting, I found it best left that way. Not so with other preserves and jams like strawberry. Sizzling Strawberry-Habanero Jam (page 128) has become a best seller in a town of formerly adverse-to-heat palates.

CANNING NOTES

- **This is an acidified but sugar-saturated hot-pack recipe.**
- **No pH testing is required.**
- **This recipe makes 9+ half-pint jars; half pints are best suited for this recipe.**
- **This recipe can be doubled but not halved.**

INGREDIENTS

5 cups finely chopped apricots
¼ cup seeded, deveined, and finely chopped jalapeños*
2 tablespoons freshly squeezed lemon juice
2 tablespoons white vinegar
½ tablespoon butter
1 pack pectin
½ tablespoon butter
7 cups sugar

DIRECTIONS

Place the fruit, peppers, juice, and vinegar in a nonreactive pot; add the butter and pectin, and mix well. Over high heat, bring to a rolling boil. Add the sugar and return to a rolling boil. Start timing for 2 minutes, checking for proper signs of jelling after 1 minute. When ready, pour into sterile jars, seal, and invert for 2 minutes only.

Seeds and veins are the hottest parts of a pepper; leave in for added heat or substitute a hotter pepper like a serrano or chile.

SERVING SUGGESTIONS

There is absolutely nothing wrong in beginning a day with a spicy jam spread. In hot climates, a spicy breakfast makes a fierce morning sun more tolerable. Hot pepper jelly over cream cheese has long been a party staple, but this jam as a substitute works just as well if not better. An omelet folded over cream cheese and a scoop of fired-up jam can start or end a day with a note of satisfaction. And on white flaky fish or a skinless chicken breast, it's fantastic.

hot vinegars

This may be the simplest canning recipe ever created and the fastest canning ever. Consider making four quart jars while the pepper season is in full swing, two using white vinegar and two using cider vinegar. The completed product can look like a masterpiece when the peppers are positioned nicely with the colors spread around; they make attractive decorations in any kitchen. The pepper selection will determine the ultimate spiciness of the finished product. Peppers need to remain covered in vinegar. Once a jar is opened and peppers are uncovered, they should be removed or the vinegar should be separated and the peppers disposed of. Treat the reserved vinegar with the same courtesy given other vinegars—not refrigerated but stored in a dark cool place is best.

CANNING NOTES

- **This an acidified water-bath recipe.**
- **pH will be so low it is not of concern; a quick check will suffice.**
- **This recipe makes 2 quart jars; quarts and pints work best.**
- **This recipe can be halved, doubled, or multiplied.**

INGREDIENTS

1½ pounds hot peppers, many colors with various heat ratings

1½ quarts white or cider vinegar, near boiling

DIRECTIONS

Prepare the peppers by making two small incisions, one on either side of each pepper. Load the jars ¾ full with the peppers scattering in a perfusion of colors throughout. Fill with hot vinegar, loosely screw lids, and insert thermometer on a cold jar (first filled). As the peppers fill with solution, more vinegar might have to be added. Process in a water bath.

When it reaches 182 degrees F, wait 2 minutes, remove, seal, and invert for 2 minutes minimum.

SERVING SUGGESTIONS

It is rare to use this vinegar at full strength except to add a splash when sautéing or cooking. For example, when sautéing spinach with garlic and olive oil, once the spinach leaves look wet and droopy, shake a dash on top to give an excellent finish to a healthy vegetable serving. These hot vinegars are most often used diluted when mixing such items as salad dressings, when making spiced mayonnaise, or when using in canning recipes that require vinegar. Adjust the dilution to the spice tolerance of the recipe and the audience.

red hot pepper jelly

This jelly is also known as "devil's pepper jelly." These jellies have become a modern mainstay of hors d'oeuvre cuisine. When using red habaneros and red bell peppers, the finished jelly is bright red, maybe warning enough it comes from Satan's lair. As you have learned from the Scoville Scale (pages 30–31), peppers range in heat from baseline zero for the bell pepper to way beyond the habanero's 350,000. While heat varies, one facet remains very similar among all these peppers—the pH. They are not all identical but close enough where one can safely substitute one volume of pepper for another. But always keep in mind that measurement is important and safety is paramount, so NEVER exceed the total measured quantity of peppers used in a recipe.

CANNING NOTES

- This is a sugar-saturated hot-pack recipe.
- No testing is required.
- This recipe makes 6 half-pint jars; pints might not jell.
- This recipe can be doubled but not halved.

INGREDIENTS

1½ cups seeded, deveined, and finely chopped red habaneros* (about 12–15 peppers)
1 cup small-diced red bell pepper (1 large pepper)
1½ cups cider vinegar
6½ cups sugar
¼ cup lime juice
½ tablespoons butter
1 pack liquid pectin

DIRECTIONS

Put the peppers and vinegar in a nonreactive pot, bring to a boil, reduce heat, and simmer for 5 minutes.

Taking care while working with the hot liquids, put peppers and vinegar in a food processor or blender, or press through a sieve to purée. Return purée to canning pot, add remaining ingredients except pectin, and bring to a rolling boil. Add pectin and return to a full boil.

After 1½ to 2 minutes when jelling is ensured, remove from heat, and fill jars. Seal and invert for 2 minutes only.

NOTE: Although the solids have been puréed, there will be separation, with the denser portion floating to the surface. As the liquid begins to set, periodically shake each jar to mix throughout until all becomes fixed. If made correctly, the process takes about three shakes over a 10-minute period after canning.

SERVING SUGGESTIONS

The standard for pepper jellies is to plop about half a jar on top of cream cheese and surround with water crackers. But this jelly is superbly hot and might offend, so be fair and label either with a note or a flashing sign cautioning all who dare to come near.

This hot jelly complements pork chop dinners. Once chops come out of the oven or off the grill, spoon and spread a thin layer of sauce on top and allow the chops to rest before serving. The molten fire can remain on or be scraped off, leaving only subtle hints of hot and sweet.

On pork tenderloins cut an incision lengthwise

in a half-cooked loin (the deeper the cut, the hotter the finished pork) and fill with pepper jelly; then finish cooking. After the meat has rested, slice into medallions and serve. Remember, sweet kills heat so a sweet potato might go well as the carbohydrate, especially one glistening with put-up orange glaze (page 148). Consider one of the green leafs as the vegetable, maybe seasoned with corn (page 72) or hot pepper relish (page 76). It's a splendid yet simple dinner, colorful to view, and dynamite (pun intended) to eat. It's a hottie!

To attain even more heat, leave the seedpods in the peppers, or to reduce heat use or mix in milder Scoville Scale red peppers like red jalapeño or serrano.

ethiopian / eritrean berbere sauce

My first military posting was in East Africa. In Eritrea and Ethiopia, complete dinners of stews, or *zigni*, made of beef, lamb or chicken are ladled on top of and eaten off of a plate of unleavened bread called *injera*. The utensils consist of more injera torn and folded so pieces of supper can be collected, the juices sopped up, and the mouthful eaten along with the bread, much like a taco; napkins are injera, also. When a meal is complete, it is truly finished—all has been eaten and there remains literally nothing on the table.

Walking through the open-air markets of East Africa is an experience that rivals watching the grandest of Africa's animals on the savannas of the Serengeti. As colorful as a Lilly Pulitzer fabric and maybe nearly as old as Lucy (an early homopod), the smells of a cuisine, unchanged within an unbroken kingdom dating back three thousand years, hang in the air while the DNA of our most ancient genes resonant with memories of our pasts.

Berbere (pronounced bear-ah-beri) is the national spice. Each household makes its own from ingredients purchased at these markets, using the family's secret recipe. It is said that the woman with the best gets the best man. It is fiercely hot yet abounds with flavor.

This is more than canning. This is a safari among East African cuisine. Once you have made the spice, all sorts of exotic experiences await. Recipes abound in the suggested servings section, and when ready to explore further, the web offers an endless berbere thread including zigni, wat, and injera recipes.

CANNING NOTES
- This is an acidified hot-pack recipe.
- pH will be low; add vinegar to reduce below 4.3.
- This recipe makes 4 half-pint jars; 4-ounce canning jars work great also.
- This recipe can be doubled, but ensure there is plenty of ventilation.

INGREDIENTS
1 cup cayenne
2 tablespoons fenugreek
1 tablespoon coriander
2 teaspoons cardamom
1½ teaspoons allspice
1 teaspoon cinnamon
1¼ teaspoons nutmeg
½ teaspoon ground cloves
½ cup red pepper flakes
½ cup paprika
⅓ cup salt
2½ teaspoons coarsely ground pepper
2½ teaspoons cumin
1½ teaspoons turmeric
½ cup minced red onion
¼ cup mashed garlic
2 tablespoons minced ginger
1 cup red wine vinegar, divided

DIRECTIONS

In a stainless pan over low heat, add the first eight ingredients and roast for 3 minutes, mixing all the while and taking great care not to burn.

In a small canning pot with no heat place the roasted spices and the remaining ingredients, withholding half of the vinegar. Mix well but do not allow it to become thin.

The finished spice should be a paste similar to the consistency of heated peanut butter. Continue to add vinegar and mix until the correct thickness is attained. Satisfied with consistency, take a pH test to ensure the spice mixture is below 4.3.

Turn on the burner, and, while stirring constantly, rapidly bring to canning temperature of 200 degrees F before spooning into jars, all the way to the canning line, seal, and invert for 2 minutes minimum.

SERVING SUGGESTIONS

Not only can this spice be used to make zigni, or stew, it can be used as a rub on beef, lamb, chicken, and fish before, during, or after cooking. It is also used as a flavoring ingredient in such items as bean stews.

Zigni: The complexity of this stew is in the spice. This has already been accomplished. The three most common types of zigni are made with beef, lamb, or chicken. Online recipes for zigni abound, and Ethiopian cookbooks are coming into their own in the United States.

Injera: This is made with a soured batter, so it must be made a day or two in advance. It is not a difficult bread to make except the flour (*teff*) is not easy to find, although it is becoming available since it is a gluten-free grain. Many health food stores now carry it. Bob's Red Mill offers Whole Grain Teff Flour along with injera instructions.

jamaican jerk rub

This rub has been around for over a thousand years. A preparation perhaps made by the Tainos Indians, Jamaica's earliest inhabitants, the rub was used not only to flavor food but to prolong the life of meat and fish. The hot pepper of the island is a scotch bonnet, a pepper nearly as hot as a habanero but with subtle yet distinguishable flavors. Where the habanero is hot, the scotch bonnet is flavorfully hot. Keep your eyes out for scotch bonnets and, when located, make this rub. A few jars go a long, long way.

CANNING NOTES

- This is an acidified hot-pack recipe.
- Initial pH will be below 4.2; add citric acid ⅛ teaspoon at a time to lower.
- This recipe makes 6 half-pint jars; half-pint and 4-ounce canning jars work best.
- This recipe can be halved, doubled, or multiplied.

INGREDIENTS

36 scotch bonnet peppers,* ground or finely chopped
36 cloves garlic, minced
12 scallions, finely chopped
1 cup freshly squeezed lime juice
1 cup fresh thyme leaves
1 cup dark brown sugar
¾ cup finely grated gingerroot
¾ cup ground allspice
½ cup pineapple juice
½ cup minced red onion
½ cup peanut oil
½ cup honey
⅜ cup coarsely ground pepper
⅜ cup cider vinegar
¼ cup orange juice
2 tablespoons salt
2 tablespoons dried sage
2 tablespoons nutmeg
2 tablespoons cinnamon

DIRECTIONS

Place all the ingredients in a nonreactive canning pot, bring to a boil, reduce heat to medium, and, stirring often, cook until thickened to a paste about the consistency between batter and honey. Bring to a canning temperature of 200 degrees F. Check pH before ladling into sterile jars. Seal and invert for required 2 minutes minimum.

Although not as hot as the habanero, scotch bonnets are VERY hot peppers. If less heat is desired, seed and devein, or use serranos or red jalapeños. Some of the flavor will be lost, but the Caribbean sense is retained without the enormous hot!

SERVING SUGGESTIONS

This rub is not just a rub. Yes, of course it can be applied (rubbed) onto chicken, fish, beef, lamb, mutton, or goat—this last being a Jamaican favorite, and for good reason. The food is then baked, broiled, grilled, or pan-fried. As a marinade, mix 1 tablespoon or more with water or with lemon or lime juice, and then place the meat in a shallow pan or in a sealable plastic bag to allow absorption (overnight for chicken and meat, or several hours for fish). The rub can be used as a seasoning in sauces to give a Caribbean accent, and, yes, jerk rub can be used for jerking meat, a process where strips of flank steak are rubbed down with the mix and then dried in the hot sun, exposed all around on an elevated rack until there is no longer any water content within the meat. This becomes an ideal, lightweight, high-protein supplement to trail snacks when hiking, kayaking, or just plain adventuring.

hot sauce

There was a time when hot sauces were an oddity. Now we often see a bottle at the table when casually dining out. There are even boutiques that specialize in hot sauces, some carrying a thousand labels. Yes, hot sauces have reached cult status. Some would call this hot, others scalding, while the aficionado of capsaicin might only chuckle from the tickle. I have ranked the three hot sauces in this section as hot, hotter, and hottest. Simple and quick to produce, this might become the everyday sauce that replaces the tiny bottle we all used to purchase, costing between $2 and $5.

CANNING NOTES

- This is an acidified hot-pack recipe.
- pH will be low, below 4; to reduce pH, add additional vinegar.
- This recipe makes 10 half pints; hot sauce bottle suppliers are found on pages 169–70.
- This recipe can be doubled or multiplied.

INGREDIENTS

3 cups finely chopped serrano peppers* (seeded and deveined, if desired)
10 cups peeled, seeded, finely chopped, and juiced vine-ripened tomatoes
6 cups distilled vinegar
1 cup honey, or 1¼ cups sugar
1 teaspoon grated fresh gingerroot
2 sticks cinnamon (remove before canning)
½ teaspoon salt
¼ teaspoon coarsely ground pepper
¼ teaspoon ground allspice

DIRECTIONS

Place all ingredients in a nonreactive canning pot and bring a boil. Hold for 5 minutes before puréeing in a blender or a food processor.

Return to pot, check pH, and bring to a canning temperature of 190 degrees F.

Fill and seal jars and then invert for 2 minutes minimum.

*This sauce can be made hotter or less hot by the selection of other peppers.

SERVING SUGGESTIONS

To taste the difference a dash of fiery sauce can make, just purchase a can of simple chicken soup, heat it up, and taste. Add a drop and taste again. Continue with the process until the heat becomes noticeable. With each droplet, flavors will be uncovered that were formerly hidden within the soup along with the added tastes of the sauce. A dash in homemade or store-bought mayonnaise can turn "bland" into something tailored for a specific use, like chicken salad. From a dash on morning eggs to a dribble on meat, fish, or poultry, hot sauces can not only unmask many flavors but just might help keep one healthy in the process. Capsaicin, the hot agent in peppers, is known to kill cancer cells, reduce cholesterol, increase metabolic rate (i.e., burn fat), and fight inflammation. Go, hot, go!

fired fruit

Number two on the "heat parade" brings forth the tastes of fruit and sweet with heat. Created for special uses, like heating up the likes of salsas made with too little of the too hot, this is a specific hot sauce. Science continues daily to learn more about the hot ingredient capsaicin, which is responsible for the hot in peppers. It has been found that cultures around the world using hot peppers in their daily diets have fewer heart attacks or strokes. Capsaicin all but eliminates sinusitis and is now believed to significantly help with arthritis. These findings are the tip of the hot pepper berg. While research continues a dab here and a dash there, a drop on this and a squirt in soups could place hot sauce and hot pepper users on the leading edge of wellness and on the way to a longer and more fruitful life.

CANNING NOTES

- **This is an acidified hot-pack recipe.**
- **pH will be low, below 4; to further reduce, add additional vinegar.**
- **This recipe makes 8 half pints; hot sauce bottle suppliers are found on pages 169–70.**
- **This recipe can be doubled or multiplied.**

INGREDIENTS

2 cups finely chopped serranos*
1/2 cup finely chopped cayennes*
1/4 cup finely chopped habaneros*
3 cups finely chopped apricots or peaches
1 grapefruit, seeded and plugged, with all membranes removed
1 3/4 cups honey
1 cup tomato purée
1 cup cider vinegar
1/2 cup lime juice
1/2 teaspoon salt

DIRECTIONS

Place all ingredients in a nonreactive canning pot and bring a boil. Hold for 5 minutes before puréeing in a blender or a food processor. Return to pot, check pH, and bring to a canning temperature of 190 degrees F.

Fill and seal jars and then invert for 2 minutes minimum.

Eighty percent of a pepper's heat is in the seeds and veins. Seed or devein or do both for a milder sauce, or adjust peppers accordingly.

SERVING SUGGESTIONS

When children are absent, I make it a habit of adding a little heat to salsas, and this is my hot sauce of choice. The sweet goes a long way with meat, and the heat releases hidden flavors. So use it in chicken salad sandwiches and salad dressings, especially whole meal summer salads. Best advice? Use this stuff like our grandmothers used butter.

texas red hot sauce

Marty Robbins was a great yarn spinner as well as balladeer of Old West tales. His story of Texas Red and the Arizona Ranger with "the big iron on his hip" comes to mind every time I draw a bottle of this sauce. Like the young outlaw gunfighter in the song, I'm sure this recipe has taken its toll, and I would be surprised if the notches on many a label were not "one and nineteen more." It's hot, oh so hot; just like its hothead namesake, its designed to be; but it has flavor, lots of flavor, and that is something most really hot sauces are lacking.

CANNING NOTES

- **This is an acidified hot-pack recipe.**
- **pH will be low, below 4; to lower, add additional vinegar.**
- **This recipe makes 7 half pints. Hot sauce bottle suppliers are on pages 169–70.**
- **This recipe can be doubled or multiplied.**

INGREDIENTS

¾ **pound red habaneros, seeded and finely chopped**
¼ **pound red serranos, seeded and finely chopped**
8 cloves garlic, minced
3 cups peeled, seeded, chopped, and juiced plum tomatoes
½ **cup finely chopped red onion**
3 cups white vinegar
1 tablespoon mustard powder (Colman's or equivalent)
1 teaspoon ground cumin
1 teaspoon crushed dried cilantro
½ **teaspoon salt**

DIRECTIONS

Place all the ingredients in a nonreactive canning pot, bring to just under a boil, reduce heat, and allow to simmer for 10 minutes. Remove from pot and purée the sauce a cup or two at a time in a blender or food processor. Return to the rinsed canning pot, bring to the canning temperature of 190 degrees F.

Check pH before filling jars, seal, and invert for 2 minutes minimum.

SERVING SUGGESTIONS

This is a stand-alone sauce, not that it is suggested that it be drunk out of the bottle (that would make for one more notch), but the flavors are as intense as the heat and therefore are meant to be enjoyed. A drip or dash on finished eggs (fried, scrambled, or soft-boiled) is a pleasant way to kick off a hot day. Many a cowpoke I've witnessed scrape off the jalapeño pickles on a burger only to replace with a half teaspoon of searing hot sauce. Me, I drip a drop here, I drop a drip there in soups, stews, wherever my imagination takes me. The sauce never fails to add.

Texas Red Hot Sauce

fiery barbeque sauce

Barbeque sauce is big business, commercially grossing about $400 million annually across the land. It not only offers great taste but brings together families and friends, making for great backyard afternoon gatherings. The theme of sweet and meat is no better defined than with this sauce.

When creating a hot barbeque sauce, the deck is stacked against success simply because there are many good ones on shelves. But when one considers the three commercial limitations—freshness, cost, and seasonal additions—a parade of improvements will march across a palate's consideration. The sauce below should win over all captains of hot barbeque as it passes in review.

CANNING NOTES

- This is an acidified hot-pack recipe.
- pH will be at 4 or below; to reduce to 4.2, add 1 tablespoon of vinegar at a time.
- This recipe makes 6 pint jars; all jar sizes work.
- This recipe can be halved, doubled, or multiplied.

INGREDIENTS

1 cup roughly chopped sweet onion
$\frac{1}{2}$ cup peanut oil, divided
4 cups peeled, seeded, chopped, and juiced
  tomatoes
1 cup chopped hot peppers (seeded and deveined,
  if desired)*
2 tablespoons mashed garlic
24 ounces chili sauce
1 cup honey
$\frac{3}{4}$ cup (unsulfured) molasses
$\frac{3}{4}$ cup cider vinegar
$\frac{1}{2}$ cup Worcestershire sauce
$\frac{1}{2}$ cup freshly squeezed orange juice
$\frac{1}{4}$ cup butter
$\frac{1}{4}$ cup coarsely ground pepper
$\frac{1}{2}$ tablespoon salt

DIRECTIONS

Place the onion in a pan with half the peanut oil and sauté until clear.

Purée the onion, tomatoes, peppers, and garlic with the chili sauce in a food processor or blender. Pour purée into a nonreactive pot with the other ingredients, bring to 200 degrees F, and hold until the sauce thickens.

Check pH and, while still at 200 degrees F, fill sterile jars, seal, and invert for 2 minutes minimum.

Review Scoville Scale (pages 30–31) to determine pepper best suited to personal preference.

SERVING SUGGESTIONS

It's not just baby back ribs. Chicken gets barbequed, whole steers get the treatment in Texas, and whole hogs in the South. Cooking on a grill or over an open fire is a common method and produces great results, but in a low-temperature oven, CrockPot, or slow cooker, the sauce seeping into the meat produces an extraordinary result and is tough to beat as an alternative. On outside fires, on grills, or in pits, the meat should be painted often with a brush to obtain maximum results. The sauce can be used like ketchup, and it can be thinned and used as a marinade by mixing 2 tablespoons of sauce to each cup of liquid, water, orange juice, etc.—whatever the chef's pleasure. Try mixing $\frac{1}{4}$ cup to $1\frac{1}{2}$ pounds of hamburger before cooking.

garlic hot sauce

Ever since Doctor Oz mentioned that garlic is so very heart-healthy, garlic this and garlic that has been popping up everywhere. Garlic is so amazing and truly is an elixir. But it can leave garlic breath and even scented skin, and so it is that some will die of vanity rather than eat garlic. Cooked garlic doesn't affect breath, so even for those who are vanity driven, this recipe will work. Even if it didn't, my advice is "Smell a little, live a little longer!"

CANNING NOTES

- **This is an acidified hot-pack recipe.**
- **pH will be at 4 or below; to lower to 4.2, add additional vinegar.**
- **This recipe makes 6 half-pint jars; jar size does not matter.**
- **This recipe can be divided, doubled, or multiplied.**

INGREDIENTS

4 cups mashed garlic

2 cups peeled, seeded, chopped, and juiced Roma tomatoes

¼ cup seeded and chopped fresh chile or cayenne peppers

3 cups white vinegar

¼ cup olive oil

3 tablespoons honey

2 teaspoons coarsely ground pepper

1 teaspoon salt

DIRECTIONS

Place all the ingredients in a nonreactive pot, bring to 160 F, and cook for 10 minutes. Purée ingredients, return to cleaned pot, check pH, and bring temperature to 200 degrees F.

While still at 200 degrees F, fill sterile jars, seal, and invert for 2 minutes minimum.

SERVING SUGGESTIONS

Often spinach is prepared in a skillet with olive oil and chopped garlic, a process much healthier than steaming, where all the nutrients end up in the water beneath the vegetable. While working with the spinach, many chefs splash a bit of vinegar along the way with a dash of hot sauce as the sautéing nears completion. Since turning out the first bottle of this hot sauce, I sauté spinach with oil while adding splashes of garlic sauce as the vegetable cooks down.

The sauce is too hot for a salad dressing, but added as a supplement or simply added to a mixture of oil and vinegar can produce a dressing of renown. Just consider what makes a marriage with garlic. Lamb chops with the sauce dribbled over as they come off the grill or out from under the broiler are just a beginning. Try using it with shrimp. Garlic and shrimp are a natural and so are shrimp and hot sauce, so garlic hot sauce over shrimp on a bed of pasta could make a lovely end-of-day repast. It's up to the reader to fill the blank volumes in between.

— sauces, marinades, and dressings —

WHEN PREPARING A NICE DINNER, the making of these specialties is often the most time-consuming activity, but sometimes they are what can take even the simplest of servings to lofty levels. Just consider ubiquitous ketchup or a common oil-and-vinegar salad dressing! The effort to make six jars at one's leisure, often enough for twelve or more four-person meals, is not much greater than the effort spent while preparing the same for a single meal. Made with the freshest and ripest of produce in season, not always the case at dinnertime, and made without those nasty, unpronounceable chemical preservatives of store-bought, the jars will be ready and waiting. And something else, a little something about all of us: when it's already there, we do it, we'll use it, and so can unfold a splendid dinner that otherwise might have passed.

When it comes to marinating, many a time just before bed I have prepared to mix up the makings for fish or meat in a ziplock bag only to discover I was missing an ingredient. It was after two such occasions when I decided, enough! I would create a canning-safe recipe and do a year's worth on a quiet weekend morning. As I toiled, I considered, why limit these marinades to this one? Between the pages of this heading and the next, you'll receive a plethora from which to choose.

Putting up is not just for speed of preparation or quality of ingredients; canning creates, as mentioned in the introduction, an art form. Chefs in upscale restaurants take great pride in their food's presentation. There is no doubt that the visual art is pleasing. When a family sits down to a dinner of, say, ham steak, rice, and broccoli, they eat. When the same family enjoys ham steak smothered in sweet potato sauce that was preserved back in October when the tubers were coming out of the ground, wild rice topped with home-canned cherry chutney, while the steamed broccoli is drizzled with your personal lemon vinaigrette dressing, they are enjoying food art: attractive yet simple, quick to fix, and designed to tantalize taste—a sense more poignant than sight.

apricot and lime curry sauce

Chutneys were originally made to go with curry dishes because the former, with all its sweetness, took some of the heat away from the spiciness of the latter. But curry itself has a remarkable flavor, so by combining a curry powder with appropriate fruits while limiting the sugars and heat, we create a topping/baking/slow-cook sauce that produces many splendid main-course dishes, especially ones with lamb, turkey, or chicken.

CANNING NOTES

- This is an acidified hot-pack recipe.
- pH is not an issue, so testing is not required.
- This recipe makes 4 or 5 pint jars; half pints work well.
- This recipe can be halved, doubled, or multiplied.

INGREDIENTS

6 cups chopped fresh apricots (about 4½ pounds)
4 limes, peeled, sliced, seeded, and slices quartered
1 cup sugar
½ cup finely chopped crystallized ginger
1 cup tomato purée
½ cup olive oil
2 tablespoons curry powder
1 tablespoon black pepper
1 tablespoon salt
1 cup honey
¼ cup balsamic vinegar

DIRECTIONS

Place all ingredients except honey and vinegar in a nonreactive canning pot. Over medium-high heat, cook until liquids from the fruit have been released and the sauce begins to thicken. Add remaining ingredients, turn heat to high, stirring constantly, and bring to 200 degrees F. Do not allow sauce to boil.

When at the consistency of thin pancake batter, remove from heat and immediately fill sterile jars, seal, and invert for 2 minutes minimum.

SERVING SUGGESTIONS

Curried dishes are a mainstay in India. British colonial rule introduced these fantastic tastes to the rest of the world and, as the saying goes, the rest is history. Smothered over and under the skin of before baking chicken will make for great eating. For a stew, use chunks of lamb, pork, or chicken baked in the sauce in a nonreactive covered pan, Dutch oven, or slow cooker and serve over brown rice; this is a main course that will be requested over and over.

light barbeque sauce

Many locales across America have their colloquial sauce for barbequeing. My first book, *Putting Up,* has one that is about as good as it gets. It's expensive and complex to produce, but it is thick! Thick sticks better than light, and light sauces require continuous painting applications of the meat. Slow cooking and thick sauces don't usually go together because they dry out quickly, and the sugars often burn, blackening the finished product. So in this book, I decided to present a canned creation from the family tree. Light but requiring no monitoring, pork, chicken, or beef can slow-cook unattended and be ready for dinner when you are.

CANNING NOTES
- **This is an acidified hot-pack recipe.**
- **Initial pH will be below 4; if higher than 4.2, some acidic ingredient was left out.**
- **This recipe makes 6 pint jars; pints will make enough servings for four.**
- **This recipe can be divided, doubled, or multiplied.**

INGREDIENTS
4 tomatoes, seeded, squeezed, and finely chopped
2 green bell peppers, finely diced
1 to 3 hot peppers, minced (optional)
1 cup minced sweet onion
4 cups cider vinegar
1 cup chili sauce
1 cup brown sugar
½ cup freshly squeezed orange juice
½ cup butter
¼ cup Worcestershire sauce
2 tablespoons chili powder
1 tablespoon coarsely ground pepper
2 teaspoons dry mustard
2 teaspoons salt
2 slices lemon, seeded, per pint jar

DIRECTIONS
Place all ingredients except lemon slices in a nonreactive pot. Bring sauce to just below boiling or 205 degrees F. Hold for 10 minutes, stirring often to prevent burning. Perform initial pH test.

Place two lemon slices in each jar to be filled. At 200 degrees F, hot-pack in sterile jars, seal, and invert for 2 minutes minimum.

SERVING SUGGESTIONS
Growing up in a little apartment in New York City, I always got excited when, upon returning home from school, the smell of slow-cooking barbeque wafted throughout. I knew it was that day of the month destined for ribs and rice with a touch of the sauce. We usually had Brussels sprouts, but mustard greens would have been nice and kale most acceptable, or any other of the dark leafy greens would have worked equally well for that matter. Much later, when I compared death rates to rib consumption, I began using chicken, beef ribs, and even chuck roasts cut into chunks. The slow-cooking process renders tender the toughest pieces of meat while combining the many BBQ flavors into a rich, hearty meal. But do try the pork ribs at least once. They have got to be good if people are willing to give their lives to eat them!

orange glaze sauce

Simple, quick to produce, and always ready at a moment's notice, this glaze dresses chicken, duck, ham, pork chops, and sweet potatoes to the nines. The key is to use the best oranges one can buy if they cannot be personally picked. Duck a l'orange, once a favorite at fashionable restaurants, has now faded from menus. I put an end to those haunting disappointments by creating this simple recipe. Now jars sit on my pantry shelf ready to "a l'orange" anything I feel might go well with the flavors.

CANNING NOTES

- **This is an acid hot-pack recipe.**
- **pH is not an issue, so testing is not required.**
- **This recipe makes 9 half-pint jars; pints and half pints work best.**
- **This recipe can be halved, doubled, or multiplied.**

INGREDIENTS

6 cups freshly squeezed orange juice (with pulp)
¼ cup orange peel, cut into small stripes (no white pith)
½ cup peanut oil
¼ cup butter, melted
1 cup honey
¼ cup finely chopped crystallized ginger or fresh gingerroot
1½ cups sugar
1½ cups light brown sugar
1 teaspoon salt
½ cup cornstarch

DIRECTIONS

Place all ingredients except cornstarch in a nonreactive pot. Bring to 210 degrees F. Mix the cornstarch with just enough water to liquefy the starch, add to the orange sauce, and stir well. When the cornstarch thickens the mixture, immediately fill sterilized jars, seal, and invert for 2 minutes minimum.

SERVING SUGGESTIONS

The French have long ago figured that duck and orange are a natural. I often wonder if they first discovered the coupling in the Orient. Duck is fatty, preparation is long, and the birds are expensive when considering a family of four. But if there is time, money, and duck available, go for it. Stuff the bird with peeled orange wedges and when ¾ done cooking, paint the entire bird inside and out with orange glaze. Repeat every 5 minutes until the duck(s) are ready. Use some of the pan juices to season accompanying wild rice. Broccoli makes a perfect vegetable here. When served, the plate is a display of colors.

As a postscript, for Christmas dinner I served ducks stuffed with plugs of orange plus two quail, each stuffed with wild rice drizzled with the sauce. When the smaller birds inside had reached 160 degrees, I began basting the ducks with the orange sauce until time to remove from the oven. The sauce produced a dinner no one at the table will ever forget. But duck is just a beginning for this sauce.

You can also bake a sweet potato and when soft, split it open and pour in some sauce—another duo like manna from heaven!

The orange sauce works wonders painted on pork chops as they cook, or try marinating a pork tenderloin in orange juice and ¼ cup of the glaze along with a pinch of cinnamon for 24 hours in a ziplock bag. Halfway thru cooking, cut an incision ½-inch deep along the top from end to end and fill with glaze. Paint the exterior and complete cooking. Cut into medallions and serve. Garnish with a slice of orange.

The best way to approach chicken is to consider it as poor man's duck. Poor as it may be, it makes a rich feast.

steak marinade

This marinade serves a twofold purpose: to flavor steaks and to tenderize less expensive cuts. Where a rib-eye or a New York strip often costs in excess of $10 a pound, steaks costing half the price work beautifully. The acids in wine, vinegar, and apple juice do the work, tenderizing while one sleeps. Place the steaks in a ziplock bag, fill with marinade, and remove the air from the bag so the solution surrounds the meat. If using a hard container, try to inundate the meat. Refrigerate and allow to marinate for at least 48 hours (more won't hurt). Remove and broil, or plunk on the outdoor grill and use leftover marinade to baste.

CANNING NOTES
- **This is an acidified hot-pack recipe.**
- **pH will be low.**
- **This recipe makes 6+ pint jars; all size jars work fine.**
- **This recipe can be halved, doubled, or multiplied.**

INGREDIENTS
4 cups seeded, finely chopped, and juiced tomatoes
2 cups honey
2 cups Worcestershire sauce
1 cup olive oil
4 cups red wine
¼ cup finely chopped garlic
¼ cup finely chopped yellow onion
½ cup apple juice
¼ cup balsamic vinegar
2 tablespoons coarsely ground pepper

DIRECTIONS
Place all ingredients in a nonreactive canning pot and bring to canning temperature of 190 degrees F. Check pH just to make sure. Fill sterile jars, seal, and invert for 2 minutes minimum.

SERVING SUGGESTIONS
The obvious was discussed in the introduction above. A bit less obvious is that by spending less on meat (often much less), a steak can turn out even better than a more expensive cut. The shopper might consider investing some of those saved dollars and purchase slightly more expensive pure grass-fed beef. We have all learned when it comes to the heart and arteries that fish is good and beef is bad. But grass-fed beef has those same kinds of fats and Omega-3 fatty acids that fish have. Seems it is the corn that makes the bad in beef we read about so much. Beef takes the rap where maybe it should be corn. Whatever your choice, an apple a day might keep the doctor away, but I don't think that would be the same for steak, even grass-fed; but twice or thrice a month will keep those carnivore teeth we all wear quite satisfied.

steak sauce

Why have all these beautiful creations in one's pantry while a bottle of store-bought sauce is used on steaks at the table? Here's the solution. Remember, these sauces go a long way, so I have purposefully made this recipe small. If the four jars don't last the year, you're probably eating too much beef!

CANNING NOTES
- This is an acidified hot-pack recipe.
- pH will be below 4.3 if measurements are correct; to lower, add extra vinegar.
- This recipe makes 4 half-pint jars; all size jars work.
- This recipe can be doubled only.

INGREDIENTS
2 tablespoons minced garlic
3/4 cup finely chopped yellow onion
2 tablespoons olive oil
12 ounces tomato paste
3 cups peeled, seeded, finely chopped, and squeezed tomatoes
1/2 cup finely diced celery
1/2 cup diced green bell pepper
1 cup cider vinegar
1/2 cup unsulfured molasses
1 tablespoon Colman's Dry Mustard
1 teaspoon ground cloves
1 teaspoon ground allspice
1 tamarind or 1/2 lemon, peeled, seeded, and finely chopped

DIRECTIONS
In a heavy-bottom nonreactive pot, sauté the garlic and onion in the olive oil until the onion is clear. Don't rush and don't let the oil smoke. Add the tomato paste and, stirring constantly, cook over medium high for 5 minutes. This will take the tinny taste out of the canned paste.

Add the tomatoes, celery, bell pepper, and vinegar. Simmer for 30 minutes. Add the remaining ingredients and bring to just under a boil for 10 minutes. To smooth out the sauce while being mindful of handling the hot liquid, purée in a food processor or blender.

Return sauce to the canning pot, bring to canning temperature of 200 degrees F, check pH, pour into sterile jars, seal, and invert for 2 minutes minimum.

SERVING SUGGESTIONS
Steak sauce is steak sauce when it's put on top of or beside meat. If eyes end up being bigger than tummies and there is steak left over, cut into bite-size bits and store refrigerated in a mixture of equal parts steak sauce, cider vinegar, and olive oil. Have steak vinaigrette as a protein snack mid-afternoon or add to a luncheon salad.

marinara sauce

Our nation prides itself as an ethnic melting pot. They came from all over, "coming to America," as Neil Diamond sang. And they brought with them their recipes. Ethnic cooking today is often simply American.

Meatballs and spaghetti are right there at the top of the list. A real quality marinara sauce like the ones that might be found bubbling in a country kitchen pot in a small Italian village can only be created with the primary ingredient of love, an ingredient that seems to be missing from commercially prepared sauces. Marinara is the most used sauce in many households, and no wonder, considering the host of applications that can be used, from a sauce for spaghetti and pizza to the sautéing of pork chops or chicken. It is canned with ease, stores in all size jars for various applications, and is homemade, with aromas, scents, and flavors causing its waifish commercial cousin to fantasize about what he could have become.

CANNING NOTES

- This is an acidified hot-pack recipe.
- pH is critical, must be monitored, and kept below 4.3. The wine, vinegar, tomatoes, and paste are the acid forces. If pH requires lowering, add ¼ teaspoon citric acid and mix well; continue until pH is at 4.2.
- This recipe makes 6 quart jars, all jar sizes work.
- This recipe can be halved, doubled, or multiplied.

INGREDIENTS

14 pounds tomatoes, peeled and finely chopped
24 ounces tomato paste
4 cups finely chopped white onion
1 cup minced celery (tender parts of stalks only)
1 cup minced carrot
1 cup olive oil, divided
1 bell pepper, small-diced
20 cloves garlic, minced
2 cups white wine (not too dry)
1 cup balsamic vinegar
¾ cup butter
¼ cup honey
2½ tablespoons chopped, tightly packed fresh oregano
1 tablespoon chopped, tightly packed fresh basil leaves
2 teaspoons chopped, tightly packed fresh parsley
2 teaspoons salt
2 teaspoons coarsely ground pepper
6 bay leaves

DIRECTIONS

Put the tomatoes in a nonreactive pot with the tomato paste and stew for 20 minutes or until beginning to thicken. Sauté the onion, celery, and carrot in a little olive oil until the onion is clear before adding with the rest of the oil to the tomatoes along with the bell pepper. Simmer for an additional 15 minutes.

Add the remaining ingredients, bring to 200 degrees F, and hold, stirring often, until thick. Retrieve bay leaves and place one in each quart jar (or see alternative tip on page 35). Check pH and adjust if necessary (see canning notes above).

Bring to canning temperature of 205 degrees F, ladle sauce into sterile jars, seal, and invert for 2 minutes minimum.

SERVING SUGGESTIONS

Pasta with marinara sauce over the top makes quite a supper. Many consider the sauce a base from which to launch. Meatballs are well known, as in meatballs and spaghetti, but shrimp or chunks of lobster mixed into the sauce and served over linguini makes an elegant meal. With a salad on the side, one could not be wanting.

Use it as a sauce spread on pizza or in lasagna, or pour over veal as in veal parmigiana.

To make meatball subs, mix ground hamburger, finely diced onion, and a little marinara, then cook and place on a crusty hot Italian loaf split lengthwise, with slices of mozzarella or Parmesan melting inside. Ladle in hot marinara for a fork-and-knife sandwich not to be beat!

seafood lynah

In the old South, cotton might have been king but rice was what one ate. It was the primary staple along with corn. The reason was simple: there was too much humidity to successfully grow wheat.

To keep rice dishes from getting boring, families created many recipes to dress up the plain starch. I grew up in such a household, and this sauce with shrimp became a favorite rice meal; this recipe has been in the family for 150 years. But many types of fish will serve equally well. It is a simple meal and yet possesses much of what is needed to remain healthy. Later in life, I switched to brown rice and, although not quite as good, knowing the health benefits made the meal actually taste better.

CANNING NOTES
- **This is an acidified hot-pack recipe.**
- **pH will be below 4.3; if above 4.2, check acid percentage of vinegar.**
- **This recipe makes 7 half-pint jars; jar size is irrelevant.**
- **This recipe can be halved, doubled, or multiplied.**

INGREDIENTS
3 cups cider vinegar
3 cups water
¼ green bell pepper, julienned
¼ yellow bell pepper, julienned
¼ red bell pepper, julienned
½ cup light olive oil
¼ cup chili sauce
¼ cup Worcestershire sauce
1 tablespoon Colman's Dry Mustard

DIRECTIONS
Place all ingredients in a canning pot, bring to 190 degrees F, check pH, pour into sterile jars (make sure each gets a share of all colors of bell peppers), and then seal and invert for 2 minutes minimum.

SERVING SUGGESTIONS
Unlike most sauces that are made for seafood to be served over rice, this is light and gentle, addressing the ocean creatures with a delicacy that seafood deserves. Since seafood has the tendency to get rubbery and tough very quickly, cook the seafood first. To make the dinner, prepare the rice, heat the sauce to hot but not boiling before adding cooked fish (cut into bite-size pieces) and/or peeled shrimp. Stir around until the seafood is warm throughout, less than 4 minutes. Do not overcook. Serve over rice with scoops of sauce containing all ingredients. An 8-ounce jar will serve four. The meal is simple and quick, plus totally unique, which is always fun.

sweet potato sauce

The fall tuber begins coming out of the ground before the first frost, but it is not until Thanksgiving that the healthy rich sweet potato really makes its winter debut. Nutrient-rich and yet seldom seen on dinner plates unless ham is served, this neglected vegetable, cultivated maybe 5,000 years ago in Central America, should get more respect. The derivation of our word "potato" comes from the Inca word for sweet potato, *batata*. Sweet Potato Butter is in my first book, *Putting Up*, and I now add two more recipes in this volume to pay homage to our continent's most powerful super food!

CANNING NOTES
- **This is an acidified hot-pack recipe.**
- **pH must be kept under 4.2; monitor closely and reduce with additional vinegar if necessary.**
- **This recipe makes 6 half-pint jars; half pints and pints serve best.**
- **This recipe can be doubled or multiplied.**

INGREDIENTS
2 tablespoons grated fresh ginger
2 tablespoons olive oil

4 cups mashed cooked sweet potatoes
  (about 3 pounds)
¼ cup butter
2 cups apple juice
¾ cup cider vinegar
½ cup honey
½ cup light brown sugar
1 teaspoon ground cinnamon
1 teaspoon ground allspice
½ teaspoon vanilla extract
½ to 1 cup water

DIRECTIONS
Sauté ginger in olive oil until golden in color. Place all ingredients except water in a nonreactive pot and bring to 180 degrees F. Check pH and adjust with additional vinegar if necessary.

Begin adding water ¼ cup at a time while stirring. Canning the sauce thicker than thinner will increase the servings since water can be added after a jar is opened. Just the same, it will need to be thinned to fill the jars.

When the desired thickness is reached, bring to a canning temperature of 200 degrees F, ladle into sterile jars, seal, and invert for 2 minutes minimum.

SERVING SUGGESTIONS
Sweet potato sauce makes leftover turkey a looked-forward-to delight; and when visiting family or friends for Thanksgiving, there is no more thoughtful a house treat.

Heat in a saucepan, but do not boil, and add water to attain the consistency desired. Ladle over turkey. The sauce works equally well with roast chicken, which is a more common meal during the year, and I suggest not waiting until leftover parts need scarfing. Have the gravy train on the table along with the fresh out-of-the-oven steaming bird. For those who still stalk in the wild for untamed fowl, with pheasant under and sauce above, the two make a noble hunter's combination.

Serve over plain angel hair pasta and one has the simplest of meals that is both tasty and nutritious. For a ham sandwich, spare some extra fat by using sauce on one slice of bread and mayo on the other.

steve's salad dressing

For two years I've been making this dressing, running out of ingredients periodically, and having to resort to something other than what I wanted. Returning home from an expedition, I noted I still had plenty of my vinegar dressing stash but was surprised at how much more flavorful it was after curing for a week. Since that revelation, I have been putting it up in batches that last at least three months. It is not heated and does not have to be—heating damages the healthful properties of olive oil—and yet it does not have to be refrigerated. It does have to be guarded though or the neighbors might get it.

CANNING NOTES
- **This is an acid recipe.**
- **No testing is necessary.**
- **This recipe makes 1 quart.**
- **This recipe can be halved, divided, doubled, or multiplied.**

INGREDIENTS
2½ cups good-quality extra virgin olive oil
½ cup distilled or bottled water
1 cup good-quality balsamic vinegar
4 teaspoons dried Italian seasoning
2 teaspoon Colman's Dry Mustard
1 teaspoon sea salt
1½ teaspoon coarsely ground black pepper
4 packs Stevia Blend (or 4 teaspoons sugar)

DIRECTIONS
Put all in a quart jar, shake well, and store in a dark area. Shake vigorously before using. The jar never becomes vacuum-sealed, so even after it is first opened, it can be re-stored in the same dark location.

SERVING SUGGESTIONS
Nobody seems to tire of this dressing, myself included. I often enjoy a nice salad at dinner or a salad for dinner five times a week. To tender lettuces like butter lettuce, add some grated carrot, a bit of sweet or red onion, and ¼-inch squares of a hard cheese like Gruyere to make a complete salad for dinner. Add diced chicken breast or other low-fat protein. Add some dried cranberries and raisins before finishing with a sprinkle of sunflower kernels. Pour the dressing over all (a little goes a long way) and sit down to extreme satisfaction as well as health. For a luncheon bite or a mid-afternoon snack, cut an avocado in half, remove the seed and fill the hole with the dressing—bet you won't put the other half away for the next day.

— preserved staples —

AS I HAVE STATED so many times in this book, when it comes to buying fresh or sort of (as one must do out of season), even if a string bean comes from Patagonia, it might still be tastier than one that has been preserved in a pressure canner at a temperature of 240 degrees. But just the same, there are items that do not fall into this category. When the season of abundance is upon us, it is up to us to pounce upon the opportunity and, shall I say, "do the can-can," for it will pay dividends all season long. My next-door neighbors, Linda and Bob, put up a few jars of this and a few jars of that each year, but they never fail to can less than 160 quart jars of tomatoes. I mean, think about it, for what don't we use tomatoes?

canned tomatoes

I do not spend much time canning just plain fruits and vegetables, but the tomato is unique and is used in so many recipe applications I find it an important canning project. Commercially, almost all tomatoes are picked green so the sun never gets to do its sweetening magic. Time, gases, or worse replace nature's way. It is why store-bought tomatoes never even come close to those luscious red orbs plucked from a garden or purchased at a farmer's roadside stand. The put-up version of tomatoes might not compete with right-off-the-vine, but it will take the ribbon when compared to store-bought, greenhouse-grown, hydroponic, nitrogen-ripened, and commercially canned tomatoes. One word of caution: because of genetic engineering, some low-acid tomatoes with a pH around 7 do exist. Before beginning, test a tomato to make sure you have genuine tomatoes with a natural pH below 4.6.

CANNING NOTES
- **This is an acid water-bath product.**
- **pH should not be an issue but should be checked for safety's sake.**
- **This recipe will make 6 quart jars; quarts and pints work best.**
- **This recipe can be divided, doubled, or multiplied.**

INGREDIENTS
12 tablespoons freshly squeezed lemon juice (2 tablespoons per jar)
17 pounds tomatoes, peeled and cored
1½ teaspoons citric acid (¼ teaspoon per jar)

DIRECTIONS
Sterilize the jars, add lemon juice to each, and pack in the tomatoes, firmly pressing in until each jar is full to the canning line. Sprinkle the citric acid on top.

Place jars with loosely attached lids and one with a thermometer stuck through in the water-bath canner with water boiling. When water begins to boil for a second time, lower the burner to maintain water temperature at just under boiling.

Bring jar temperature to 190 degrees F, wait 2 minutes, remove, replace thermometer lid, tighten all lids, and invert for 2 minutes minimum.

SERVING SUGGESTIONS
Canned tomatoes are more a staple than a food. Throughout this book, recipes call for fresh tomatoes. Often home-canned will work fine. A perfect example is the Marinara Sauce (page 152) or Steak Sauce (page 151), while with a recipe like Tomato-Basil Soup (page 118), one would want to use just-picked fresh fruit. The key to deciding is, does the recipe have longer cooking times? If it does, the jars of put-up fresh tomatoes will work perfectly. But there remains much more we use tomatoes for throughout the year. Build a cache of ripe, sweet fruit. It will be gone by the first reds of the next crop.

herb-infused vinegar

When in season, herbs range from cheap to free if one has an herb pot or mini garden. Off season, they can be as pricey as a meal. Meanwhile, vinegars (5 percent acidity) hold their price year-round. It is as easy as one-two-three to infuse the flavors of herbs in concentration within vinegars (white and cider) for use to season other vinegars later.

CANNING NOTES
- **This is an acidified hot-pack recipe.**
- **pH is not an issue if measurements are correct.**
- **The recipe makes 1 or more pint jars.**
- **The recipe can be doubled or multiplied.**

INGREDIENTS
½ cup roughly chopped, tightly packed herbs
   (basil, oregano, thyme, etc.), one or more
2 cups cider or distilled vinegar

DIRECTIONS
Heat the vinegar to boiling, add the herbs, stir well, and fill the sterile pint jar. Seal and invert for 2 minutes minimum.

SERVING SUGGESTIONS
This staple is used to give other vinegars herb flavoring. It can be used undiluted to splash while cooking, thus adding both an acid and a seasoning in a teaspoon. By adding one or two parts of infused to six or seven parts of plain vinegar, either cider or white, the new can be used to enhance the vinegar in salad dressings, added to mayonnaise as a thinner, used as the acid when making it, and used to season vinegar when canning. Diluted, these quick and simple jars of herb vinegar rapidly become your gourmet kitchen necessity just like salt and pepper.

afterthoughts

More Canning

A pantry can now be filled (or one might have to be built!). Former no-frills home dining is about to end. Dining will become exciting, and food costs can plummet while health rises. If you remain excited after the first five recipes are on the shelf, then a new adventure has unfolded.

The serving suggestions provided with each recipe are merely a handful. Many more await your discovery and creativity. Each jar in every pantry is limited only by imagination. More recipes are available. Like this current volume, my first book, *Putting Up*, has over sixty additional recipes as well as more detailed information on the canning process. Once one has completed ten or fifteen recipes, it's easy to understand the science behind it.

Preserving one's own recipes is no different than these. Safe canning, controlled by the few simple criteria detailed in the first chapter, will ensure that a personal recipe is safe. This and selecting choice produce that stands up well under heat will ultimately determine whether a recipe works. Sometimes added experimentation will be needed to get the flavors just right; but if the acid level is correct, the canning temperature is married to the acid level, the canning jar and lid are sterile, a good vacuum is created, and the product is tested just before canning and again 24 hours later, then the finished product will be safe.

Gift Giving

When visiting or going to dinner, there is no finer gift than giving a jar of a home put-up recipe, for it represents time, toil, and best efforts. It speaks so much louder than the obligatory bottle of wine or purchased flowers. When presenting jars as gifts, consider dressing them up to make them extra special. Visit a fabric store. Select thin fabrics like calicos. The material comes in many colors and patterns, some even seasonal for an added touch. Using pinking shears, cut the fabric into 4-inch squares (or circles if you enjoy labor-intensive tasks). Carefully remove the ring part of the two-piece lid and fold the selected fabric over the top of the jar; then, without forcing, gently reattach the ring. It is important not to break the seal. Gentle is the key. One might even make and add a little label. It can be written by hand, or it can be printed on a computer using 2 x 4-inch stick-on labels, available at most office supply stores.

Here are a few more ideas. Most craft stores sell unfinished baskets. A few jars with seasonal fabric on the lids, arranged inside a small wicker basket that has been spray-painted for the occasion, goes deep into recipients' hearts as well as their stomachs. For simple gifts with an impact, try tying a helium balloon to a jar. Or wrap a jar in a bow or raffia. Options are endless.

Mango Chutney
for
Linda & Bob
made 7/21/10

Keeping Expenses Low

Canning is inexpensive when compared to alternatives. Still there are ways one can save additional money while still enjoying the complete canning experience. Here are some:

Glass

Jars are expensive but are reusable. Once a jar is depleted, inspect it to ensure it is not damaged. Hold it up to a good light, inspect for cracks, and carefully run your finger around the rim to check for chipping. Discard those that are damaged. Wash those that are intact (which will be most of them since these are tough pieces of glass made to expand and contract because of rapid heat changes) and return to the original case, inverted for the next canning session.

Jar prices are all over the place. I often see cases of jars for $7.99 in a grocery store that I have just purchased at Walmart for $4.99. Then there are jars with frilly flowers embossed on the outside; these cost more and offer nothing as an advantage. The least expensive outlet in this local area is Big Lots. Their prices are frequently less than what a commercial cannery pays directly from the manufacturer. Find a local discounter. Or better yet, find one and make them a deal on a bulk purchase. And if they carry jars, they most likely have other canning supplies as well, all for much less!

Lids

Lid centers are not reusable. The flat disc part of the two-piece lid can only be used once, but the good news is that this part of the lid is the least inexpensive, at some discount stores less than a dime. On the other hand, lid rings (the outer band) can be used over and over. Plus, they do not have to be left on jars after the sealing process is complete. If you choose to store your finished recipes without rings once the jars have cooled completely, carefully remove and store after a minimum of 24 hours.

Pectin

Pectin is expensive, and the range of pricing for identical little boxes is incredible. If planning on making more than a run or five of preserves, I strongly suggest buying bulk pectin. It is so much less expensive, and it will last at least two seasons when stored properly. Pacific Pectin (pacificpectin.com) makes a quality product, and they have a staff to assist with questions. Buying in bulk saves about two-thirds.

Produce

Most of us don't have fields or gardens from which we pluck our produce. This means we have to buy it. When the season of plenty is in full swing, prices are at their lowest point, and there is no better time to preserve. Canning six quarts of tomatoes during peak tomato season might cost about $7, plus jars. Six months later, the same exercise might cost over $35. Always put up in season, preferably in the middle when prices are often at their lowest.

Bulk Purchasing

Purchasing in bulk can save a bundle. Opening an account with a discount bulk seller like Costco or Sam's Club will pay for itself just with items like coarsely ground black pepper, sugar, and vinegar.

Miscellaneous Savings

pH PAPER: pH paper is not expensive, and rolls (the better choice) are far less expensive than strips. The least expensive way to purchase is directly from the manufacturer, Hydrion (see Resource Section, page 170). One roll of the paper needed, narrow range 3.4 to 4.8 paper, is about $5 and will last the year; unfortunately, one has to purchase five rolls. One order among several friends works well.

SPICES: Once into canning, one will use a lot of certain spices. Three that come to mind are crystallized ginger, mustard seed, and celery seed. Packaging and producer profit are your biggest costs. Often buying these items at a store that has a bulk section saves a ton of money. Purchasing 2-cup plastic tubs of these items saves 50 to 90 percent when compared to little spice jars.

SALT: Canning salt is canning-specific. The boxes are in grocery stores, usually near the jars. Very expensive! Morton's produces 25-pound bags of pure salt; that's what canning salt is—pure. For around $4 retail, one has the salt needed for the year! If your local grocer does not carry this product, have him order it; we all know he does business with Morton's.

Making Canning a Career

One memorable day I had this year was when a young lady came up to me while I was signing books and asked if I remembered her. She was young and attractive, so of course I said yes. Fortunately, she went ahead and tried to refresh my memory; seems she had bought my book the summer before at a farmers market. While I signed it, and for some time after, she had picked my brain about the commercial aspects of canning. Well, to make a long story fit between these pages, she told me of her success. And, oh boy, was it a success—with newspaper articles and stories of crowds around her market booth, along with a tidy income. As she was leaving, she thanked me for pointing her toward her life's career. It was one of my year's most rewarding days.

Going to the Source

Every day, my first chore is to answer e-mails originating from all around the globe. None are stupid. One cannot ask a silly question when dealing with a subject that could produce lethal consequences. I try to answer all questions expeditiously. It doesn't always happen, but I try. Visit my two websites: puttingup.com and stevedowdney.com.

resources

Canning is a tradition that now spans five generations, so the art is well entrenched within our society. Consequently, much of the equipment needed is available locally. Walmart, Kmart, and most local hardware stores like Ace cater to the home canner and all things related. Water-bath systems, pots, jars, and most other canning supplies can be found locally at places like these. As a minimum, many regional grocery stores carry jars, pectin, and citric acid. Metropolitan dwellers may have more difficulty, but a weekend drive to a more rural setting will be good for the soul, and one will probably find what he seeks.

Many upscale kitchen stores carry a variety of canning-friendly products like quality pots, measuring items, stirring utensils, and scales. These are nice to own, and I admit I have a few, but the less expensive can work equally well. Follow the guidelines in chapter one. It's inexpensive but sound starting guidance. Most importantly, shop and purchase locally whenever possible; it's your community, help keep your businesses strong and your neighbors employed. Also, shipping is very expensive, and many companies consider their shipping department a major profit center. Bottom line, you end up being charged much more than their cost of packaging and freight. This mentality has become so obnoxious that when it is outlandishly obvious to me, I refuse to do business with such companies.

Equipment

Local
Ace Hardware, Kmart, Walmart

Mail Order
All American Canner
www.allamericancanner.com
1-800-251-8824

Canning Pantry
www.canningpantry.com
1-800-285-9044

Canning Supply Co.
www.canningsupply.com
1-888-612-1950

Kitchen Krafts
www.kitchenkrafts.com
1-800-298-5389

Supplies

Canning Jars/Lids
Local grocery store, hardware stores, Walmart, bulk discounters like Big Lots; or order from above and pay big shipping fees

Specialized Glass
Berlin Container
www.berlinpackaging.com
1-800-2-Berlin
1-800-223-7546

Freund Container & Supply
www.freundcontainer.com
1-877-637-3863

SKS Bottle & Packaging
www.sks-bottle.com
1-518-880-6980

pH Paper/Meters

Micro Essential Laboratory Hydrion
www.microessentiallab.com
1-718-338-3618

The Science Company
www.sciencecompany.com
1-800-372-6726

Spices

A1 Spice World
www.a1spiceworld.com
1-516-801-2132

The Great American Spice Co.
www.americanspice.com
1-877-6SPICE
9 1-877-677-4239

Vanns Spices
www.vannsspices.com
1-800-583-1693

Metric Conversion Chart

VOLUME MEASUREMENTS		WEIGHT MEASUREMENTS		TEMPERATURE CONVERSION	
U.S.	METRIC	U.S.	METRIC	FAHRENHEIT	CELSIUS
1 teaspoon	5 ml	½ ounce	15 g	250	120
1 tablespoon	15 ml	1 ounce	30 g	300	150
¼ cup	60 ml	3 ounces	90 g	325	160
⅓ cup	75 ml	4 ounces	115 y	350	180
½ cup	125 ml	8 ounces	225 g	375	190
⅔ cup	150 ml	12 ounces	350 g	400	200
¾ cup	175 ml	1 pound	450 g	425	220
1 cup	250 ml	2¼ pounds	1 kg	450	230

index

onion (red), use of, in recipes, 60, 68, 70, 73, 80, 82, 88, 90, 96, 106, 116, 134, 136, 140

onion (sweet), use of, in recipes, 62, 75, 83, 122, 142, 147

onion (white), use of, in recipes, 86, 104, 105, 108, 118, 152

onion (yellow), use of, in recipes, 76, 84, 126, 150, 151

Orange and Date Chutney, 82

Orange-Fig Marmalade, 44

Orange Glaze Sauce, 148–49

Orange Relish, Cranberry-, 75

oranges/juice/zest, use of, in recipes, 42, 44, 47, 52, 75, 82, 83, 86, 112, 114, 116, 120, 142, 147, 148

P

Peach Relish, 70

peaches, use of, in recipes, 70, 139

peas, black-eyed, use of, in recipes, 106

Pepper Jelly, Devil's, 132–33

Pepper Jelly, Onion-, 60

Pepper Jelly, Rainbow, 49

Pepper Jelly, Red Hot, 132–33

Pepper Relish, Hot, 76

peppers, hot, 30–31; handling caution, 31, 127; pepper hotness, varying, 138; seedpods, seeds, and veins of, 130, 133, 137, 139

peppers, hot, use of, in recipes, 49, 60, 70, 76, 80, 88, 100, 104, 105, 108, 126–43, 147. *See also* bell peppers

Persimmon Jelly, 59

pH meter, 25

pH paper, 24

pH testing. *See* acidity (pH), measuring/testing

Pickled Brussels Sprouts, 98–99

Pickled Jalapeños, 126–27

pickles, recipes for, 94–101, 126–27

pickling cucumbers, 101

pineapple, use of, in recipes, 90

preserves: definition of, 40; recipes for, 55, 56

preserving methods, 14–15

Prickly Pear Cactus Jelly, 53

prickly pear cactus juice, how to make, 53

produce, selecting, 21

Putting Up, 11, 12, 13, 14, 30, 75, 76, 100, 125, 147, 155

Putting Up More, 12

R

radishes, use of, in recipes, 94

Rainbow Pepper Jelly, 49

raisins, use of, in recipes, 80, 82, 83, 84, 86

recipe preparation, 22

Red Cherry Preserves, 56

Red Hot Pepper Jelly, 132–33

resources: equipment, pH paper/meters, spices, supplies, 169–70

Rub, Jamaican Jerk, 136–37

S

safe canning practices, 15–18

Salad Dressing, Steve's, 156

salt, canning, 26–27

sauces, recipes for, 138, 140, 142, 143, 146, 147, 148–49, 151, 152, 154, 155

savings: pH paper, salt, spices, 167–68

scallions, use of, in recipes, 136

scotch bonnet peppers, use of, in recipes, 136

Scoville Scale, 30–31, 76, 126, 132, 133, 142

Seafood Chutney, 90–91

Seafood Lynah, 154

seafood, recipes for, 90–91, 120–21, 154. *See also* fish

seal/vacuum, creating a, 16, 25

serrano peppers, use of, in recipes, 138, 139, 140

"small batch" cannery, 13

squash, butternut, use of, in recipes, 114

squash, summer, use of, in recipes, 96

squash, yellow, use of, in recipes, 88

Steak Marinade, 150

Steak Sauce, 151, 160